YouTube Mastery

The Ultimate In-Depth Guide to Building
a Thriving YouTube Channel

Matthew Wheeler

ISBN-13: 9798375685748

Printed in the United States of America

DEDICATION

Dedicated to Taylor, my rock and my biggest cheerleader.

From the very first day that I started dreaming about creating a successful YouTube channel and education business, you have been by my side, offering unwavering support, encouragement, and love. You have been my sounding board for ideas, my editor, my motivational anchor, and my biggest fan, always eager to share my content with anyone who will listen.

I am so grateful for the sacrifices you have made and the time you have invested to help me make this dream a reality. You continually give me the confidence to pursue my passion and the strength to face any obstacle that comes my way.

This book is a testament to the current step in our journey together and all the ones taken before, and I am honored to dedicate it to you. Thank you for being my partner in life, love, and business. I love you more than words can express.

With love and gratitude,
Matthew Wheeler

"Punch fear in the face, punch perfectionism in the face, and press record."

-Sean Cannell

CONTENTS

Introduction   Pg # 1

1   Defining your Niche   Pg # 3

2   Creating a Content Plan   Pg # 9

3   Optimizing your Channel   Pg # 18

4   Investing in Equipment   Pg # 27

5   Creating Engaging Content   Pg # 34

6   Promoting your Channel   Pg # 41

7   Monetizing your Channel   Pg # 48

8   Staying Up-to-date and Experimenting   Pg # 55

        Conclusion   Pg # 62

        Checklist   Pg # 68

        Links to Resources   Pg # 90

        Appendix A   Pg # 121

        References   Pg # 122

        Afterword   Pg # 126

Introduction:

YouTube is one of the most widely used platforms for creators to share their content, connect with their audience and even turn their passion into a career. With over 2 billion monthly active users, YouTube offers an unprecedented opportunity for creators to connect with audiences around the world and make an impact.

The benefits of creating a YouTube channel are numerous. First, it allows creators to share their passion and expertise with a global audience. Regardless of the niche, whether it is cooking, beauty, gaming, or anything else, YouTube provides an opportunity for creators to build a community of individuals who share their interests and engage with their content.

Furthermore, YouTube also offers creators the chance to turn their hobby into a career. With the right strategy, creators can monetize their channel through ads, sponsorships, collaborations and even make a sustainable income. In fact, many creators have been able to turn their YouTube channel into a full-time job, with the platform serving as a stepping stone to other opportunities like book deals, speaking engagements and more.

The current state of YouTube is strong and the potential for growth and success is tremendous. The platform is continuously evolving, with new features and opportunities for creators to take advantage of. YouTube's algorithm is also constantly changing, making it easier for creators to reach and engage with their audiences. With the right approach and by following best practices, creators can grow their channel and achieve success on the platform.

This guide is designed to walk you through the process of starting a YouTube channel from scratch, from choosing your niche to creating a content plan, optimizing your channel, and monetizing your content. We will provide tips and strategies for growing your audience, staying up-to-date with the latest trends, and experimenting to find what works best for your channel. We will also show you how you can turn your hobby or passion into a career and help you achieve success on the world's largest video sharing platform.

In this guide, you will learn how to:
- Choose a niche that aligns with your interests and expertise
- Plan out your content in advance and make sure it aligns with your niche
- Set up your channel for success, with a catchy title, a good description and a profile picture that represents your brand.
- Invest in good quality equipment
- Create engaging, informative, and entertaining content
- Use social media and other platforms to promote your channel and grow your audience
- Monetize your channel through ads, sponsorships, and collaborations
- Stay up-to-date with the latest trends and algorithms on YouTube and always be willing to experiment and try new things to see what works best for your channel.

Creating a YouTube channel is a great way to share your passion and expertise with the world, connect with like-minded individuals, and potentially turn your hobby into a career. With the right approach, tools, and strategies, you can be on your way to building a successful channel that makes an impact and reaches your goals. So, let's dive in, get started, and bring your ideas to life on YouTube!

Chapter 1: Defining your Niche

Starting a YouTube channel can be an exciting and rewarding experience, but it's important to remember that success doesn't come overnight. One of the key elements to creating a successful YouTube channel is defining your niche. In this chapter, we will discuss how to choose a niche that aligns with your interests and expertise, the importance of having a unique niche in a crowded market, researching the demand for your niche and understanding your target audience, and identifying and analyzing the competition within your niche.

First and foremost, it's important to choose a niche that aligns with your interests and expertise . This is crucial for the success of your YouTube channel because it will make it easier for you to create content and stay motivated. When choosing a niche, it's important to consider your passions and interests, and also your expertise. Think about what you enjoy doing and what you're good at. It can be easy to get caught up in trends and popular niches, but it's important to find a balance between your interests and expertise and choose a niche that allows you to share your knowledge and skills in a unique and engaging way.

For example, if you have a passion for cooking and have experience working as a professional chef, your niche could be creating cooking videos that focus on teaching viewers how to cook gourmet meals at home; a cooking channel might be a good fit for you. Similarly, if you have a background in photography and enjoy taking pictures, then a photography channel might be a great option. It's also important to consider your expertise when choosing a niche. Think about what you know and what you're good at. If you're an expert in a particular field, like marketing or finance, then creating a channel that focuses on that topic could be a great way to share your expertise and build an audience. The key is to find a balance between your interests and expertise and choose a niche that allows you to share your knowledge and skills in a unique and engaging way.

Additionally, it's important to consider the demand for your chosen niche. Research your niche and find out if there is a significant audience for the type of content you want to create. Look at the number of existing channels in your niche and see if there is an opportunity for you to stand out by providing unique and valuable content. Also, research on the target audience you want to reach, understand their demographics and tailor your content to meet their needs. Once you've found a niche with good demand, it's also important to consider the competition within that niche. Analyze the existing channels in your niche and see what they're doing well and what they're not. Look at their content, their audience, and their engagement. Identify the gaps in the market and think about how you can fill those gaps with your own unique approach. By understanding the competition, you can position yourself in a way that sets you apart and makes you stand out. Take the time to carefully research and choose the right niche for your channel, and you'll be setting yourself up for success and creating content that you're passionate about and your audience will love.

The next important aspect is having a unique niche in a crowded market. A crowded market refers to a niche that has a high number of existing channels and creators, making it more difficult for new channels to stand out and gain traction. When you have a unique niche, it makes it easier for you to differentiate yourself from the competition and attract the attention of your target audience. It also allows you to establish yourself as an authority in your niche and build a loyal following. Having a unique niche can also increase your chances of monetizing your channel more quickly, as you will have a specific audience that is interested in your content.

One way to find a unique niche is to identify an area of interest that is underrepresented on YouTube. For example, if you're an expert in a specific type of photography, like nature photography or macro photography, you could create a channel that focuses on that specific niche. Or, if you want to create a YouTube channel about fitness, instead of just creating workout videos, you could focus on a specific aspect of fitness, such as Yoga for seniors or Mindfulness and meditation for fitness. This allows you to stand out and attract a specific audience that is interested in that type of content. Another way to find a unique niche is to combine multiple areas of interest. For example, if you're interested in cooking and traveling, you could create a channel that focuses on food from around the world. This allows you to combine your interests and attract an audience that is interested in both cooking and traveling.

Yet another way to find a unique niche is to create a unique format of content. If you're a musician and you want to start a YouTube channel, you could create a channel that focuses on music lessons and tutorials, but you could make it more unique by creating a show format, where you have a guest musician each episode and you both teach a lesson together. This allows you to stand out from other music channels and attract an audience that is interested in learning from multiple musicians. It's important to note that having a unique niche doesn't mean that you have to be the only one in your niche, but it does mean that you have to have a unique approach, a unique format or a unique angle that makes you different from the existing channels. By taking the time to find a unique niche, you'll be setting yourself up for success and creating content that sets you apart from the competition.

Once you've defined your niche, it's important to research the demand for your niche and understand your target audience. Researching the demand for your niche and understanding your target audience are key elements in the success of your YouTube channel. By understanding the demand for your niche and your target audience, you'll be able to create content that is relevant, engaging and meets the needs of your audience. Researching the demand for your niche involves understanding the current market trends and identifying the areas of interest that are currently popular on YouTube. This can be done by analyzing the existing channels in your niche and identifying the types of content that are performing well. You can use tools such as Google Trends, YouTube's search bar, YouTube Analytics, YouTube

Keyword Planner, Social Blade, VidIQ, TubeBuddy, and/or other social media analytics tools to gather data about your niche. (There will be links to these tools later in the action plan toward the end of the book.) Understanding your target audience involves identifying the demographics of the people who are most likely to be interested in your content, as well as understanding their interests, needs and pain points, and their behavior. This information can be gathered by researching the audience of existing channels in your niche, conducting surveys and focus groups, and analyzing the engagement on your own content.

Once you have a good understanding of the demand for your niche, you can then focus on understanding your target audience. This involves identifying the demographics of the people who are most likely to be interested in your content. For example, if you're creating a channel that focuses on parenting, your target audience would likely be parents or parents-to-be. Understanding the demographics of your target audience will help you to create content that is relevant and engaging to them. It's also important to understand the needs and pain points of your target audience. You should perform research on what they are looking for in terms of content, what their interests are, what they are struggling with, what are the questions they are trying to answer. By understanding their needs and pain points, you'll be able to create content that addresses those specific needs and pain points and provides value to your audience. Another key aspect of understanding your target audience is understanding their behavior. This includes understanding the type of content they are most likely to engage with, the time of day they are most active on YouTube, and the platforms they use to discover new content. By understanding your target audience's behavior, you'll be able to create content that is tailored to their preferences and reach them at the right time and in the right way.

Research the demand for your niche and understand your target audience, as these are key elements in the success of your YouTube channel. By understanding the demand for your niche, you'll be able to create content that is relevant and meets the needs of your audience. By understanding your target audience, you'll be able to create content that is tailored to their preferences and reaches them at the right time, in the right way, providing valuable content that addresses their pain points and interests.

Finally, it's important to identify and analyze the competition within your niche. By understanding the competition, you'll be able to identify opportunities, set realistic goals, and create a strategy that sets you apart from the competition. This includes analyzing the strengths and weaknesses of existing channels in your niche, identifying the gaps in the market, and creating a strategy that sets your channel apart from the competition. This can be done by studying the content, engagement, and audience of existing channels, as well as identifying any missing or under-served topics within your niche.

The first step in identifying and analyzing the competition within your niche is to research existing channels in your niche. Look at the number of subscribers, views, and engagement on their videos. Also, take a look at their content, the topics they cover, and the format they use to deliver their content. This will give you an idea of the current state of your niche and the types of content that are resonating with the audience.

Once you have a good understanding of the existing channels in your niche, you should analyze their strengths and weaknesses. Identify what they are doing well and what they are not. Look at their audience, their engagement, and their monetization strategies. This will give you an idea of the areas where you can improve and stand out from the competition.

It's also important to identify the gaps in the market. Look for areas where there is a lack of content or where existing channels are not providing enough value to the audience. This is an opportunity for you to fill the gap with your unique approach, a unique format or a unique angle.

By analyzing the competition, you can also set realistic goals for your channel. Look at the number of subscribers and views that the existing channels in your niche have and use that as a benchmark for your own channel. Additionally, by understanding the competition, you'll be able to identify opportunities, set realistic goals, and create a strategy that sets you apart from the competition. This can include creating unique content, a unique format or a unique angle, or a unique approach to monetization. Furthermore, by identifying the gaps in the market, you can fill it with your unique approach, format or angle, and make your channel stand out in the crowded market.

In conclusion, defining your niche is a very important step in creating a successful YouTube channel. It's important to choose a niche that aligns with your interests and expertise, have a unique niche in a crowded market, research the demand for your niche and understand your target audience, and identify and analyze the competition within your niche. Take the time to define your niche, and you'll be able to create content that resonates with your target audience, and set yourself apart from the competition. Remember, success on YouTube takes time and effort, but by following these steps and staying true to your niche, you'll be well on your way to creating a successful and sustainable YouTube channel.

Chapter 2: Creating a Content Plan:

Understanding the importance of and creating a content plan is a crucial step in building a successful YouTube channel. It allows you to keep your audience engaged, stay organized, and on schedule, which is essential in maintaining consistency and regular uploads. This plan should include the type of content you'll be creating, the frequency of uploads, and the overall theme or message of your channel. By having a content plan, you can ensure that your content is consistent and aligns with your niche and target audience. In this chapter, we'll go over how to plan out your content in advance, the importance of consistency and regular uploads, and how to stay organized and on schedule, which are all key when it comes to building a loyal audience. Regularly uploading new and consistent content will keep your viewers engaged and coming back for more.. We'll also discuss how to identify the type of content that works best for your audience and niche and how to set realistic and achievable content creation and upload goals.

First, let's talk about how to plan out your content in advance. Planning ahead allows you to be more strategic about the content you're creating and how it aligns with your overall goals for your channel. When it comes to creating a content plan for your YouTube channel, the first step is to determine the type of content you want to create and how often you want to upload it. This is crucial for maintaining consistency and regularity on your channel, which is essential for building and retaining an audience. One way to plan out your content in advance is to create a content calendar. This can be as simple as a spreadsheet, a digital calendar, or a physical planner, or a more advanced tool like Trello, Monday, or Asana. (There will be links to these tools later in the action plan toward the end of the book.) Your content calendar should include the topics you'll be covering, the types of content you'll be creating (e.g. video, blog post, live stream),the dates they'll be published, and any other relevant information, such as keywords or hashtags. By having a content calendar, you can easily see what content is coming up and make adjustments as needed. It also allows you to plan in advance for holidays or special events that may affect your content schedule. It's also helpful to plan out your content in advance so that you have time to gather all necessary materials and equipment, if needed.

One way to stay organized and on schedule is to set specific content creation and upload goals. For example, you may want to upload one video per week or create a certain number of blog posts per month. By setting these goals, you'll have a clear idea of what needs to be done and when it needs to be done. It's also important to hold yourself accountable for meeting these goals and to track your progress over time. Another way to stay organized is to use a project management tool. These tools allow you to collaborate with a team, if you have one, and keep track of deadlines, tasks, and progress. Some popular project management tools include Trello, Asana, and Monday. (There will be links to these tools later in the action plan toward the end of the book.)

In addition, it's important to identify the type of content that works best for your audience and niche, which we'll cover in more detail later in this chapter. Not all content formats will be suitable for all channels, so it's important to experiment and test different types of content to see what resonates with your audience. For example, if you're in the beauty niche, you may want to focus on creating makeup tutorial videos, while a cooking channel may focus on recipe videos or cooking tutorials. On the other hand, if your niche is centered around travel, then vlogs and travel guides may be more appropriate. It's important to consider your audience's preferences and what type of content will best engage and entertain them. By understanding the content that works best for your channel, you can create a content plan that is tailored to your audience's preferences.

When creating your content calendar, it's also important to set realistic and achievable content creation and upload goals. This will help you stay on track and motivated, and it will also give you a clear understanding of how much content you need to create and when it needs to be ready. For example, if you plan on uploading a new video every Monday, Wednesday, and Friday, then you should aim to have at least 3 videos ready to go each week. Additionally, you should also consider incorporating different types of content into your calendar to keep things interesting for your audience.

This can include live streams, Q&A sessions, and challenge videos, which can help to break up the monotony and add variety to your channel.

Consistency and regular uploads are essential for growing your audience and building your brand. By having a content calendar in place, you can ensure that you are regularly uploading new content for your audience to engage with. When viewers see that you're consistently uploading new content, This helps in building a loyal audience as they're more likely to subscribe to your channel and tune in for future uploads if they know when to expect new content. It's important to find a schedule that works for you and your audience and stick to it. If you're just starting out, you may want to start with one video per week and increase the frequency as your channel grows. It's also important to note that the type of content you're creating will also play a role in determining your upload schedule. For example, if you're creating vlogs, it may make sense to upload on a daily basis, whereas if you're creating more in-depth, research-based content, it may make sense to upload on a weekly or bi-weekly basis.

First and foremost, consistency in terms of upload schedule helps to keep your audience engaged and informed. If your viewers know when to expect new content from you, they are more likely to tune in and watch. This is especially true if you can establish a regular upload schedule that they can count on. For example, if you upload a new video every Monday and Thursday at the same time, your audience will start to look forward to those days and will be more likely to watch your videos live.

Additionally, consistency in terms of the frequency of your uploads can also help you grow your audience by making it easier for viewers to discover your content. YouTube's algorithm favors channels that upload regularly and consistently, so the more videos you have, the more opportunities you have to be discovered by new viewers. This is especially true if your channel is new and you're trying to build an audience from scratch.

Consistency also plays a role in creating a sense of reliability in the eyes of your audience. If viewers can count on your channel to consistently upload high-quality content, they are more likely to trust you and see you as a credible source of information or entertainment. This can lead to increased engagement and loyalty, which can help you grow your audience. To restate, consistency in terms of the quality of your content is very important. If your videos are poorly produced or lack attention to detail, it will be hard to keep your audience engaged. On the other hand, if your videos are well-produced, engaging and informative, your audience will be more likely to stick around and watch more of your content.

Furthermore, Consistency in terms of the type of content you upload is also important. Your audience will come to expect a certain type of content from you, and if you deviate too far from that, they may become confused or lose interest. For example, if you are known for uploading cooking videos, your audience will expect cooking-related content from you, if you suddenly start uploading travel videos, your audience may not understand the shift and may lose interest in your channel. It's important to note that consistency in your content doesn't mean that you should only stick to one type of content or format, but rather that you should be very consistent in the themes and topics that you cover. This will help you build a loyal audience that is engaged with your content and interested in what you have to say.

Staying organized and on schedule is crucial for maintaining consistency and regular uploads. This includes not only planning out or outlining the types of content you will create and when you will upload them, but also setting reminders for filming and editing, so you don't fall behind schedule. It's also helpful to keep a running list of content ideas, so you don't run out of ideas, and to track your progress by keeping a record of the number of views and engagement on your videos. This is where using a project management tool such as Trello, Asana, or Monday really shines, as these tools allow you to keep track of deadlines, assign tasks, and collaborate with team members as your organization grows from just you to two, three, ten, or even more people. Even just by yourself, this will help you to stay on top of your content creation schedule, and ensure that all the necessary steps are taken before publishing a video.

Another important aspect of staying on schedule is to be flexible and open to change. This means that you should be willing to adjust your content calendar as needed. For example, if a video does not perform as well as you had hoped, you should be willing to change your approach or try something new. Additionally, if a certain type of content is particularly popular with your audience, you should consider producing more of that type of content. Being flexible and open to change will allow you to adapt to the needs of your audience and stay on schedule.

In addition, time management is a key aspect of staying on schedule. This means that you should prioritize your tasks and focus on the most important ones first. It's also important to set aside dedicated time for creating and uploading content, and to avoid distractions during this time. By managing your time effectively, you can ensure that you are able to consistently upload high-quality content on schedule.

Identifying the type of content that works best for your audience and niche is important for maintaining engagement and growing your audience. Creating content that resonates with your target audience is crucial for growing your YouTube channel. Understanding what type of content is most appealing to your audience will help you to create content that they will engage with, share, and ultimately keep coming back to watch.

To identify the type of content that works best for your audience, it's important to conduct research on your target audience. This can include surveys, focus groups, and analyzing data from your existing audience. Through this research, you can learn about your audience's interests, demographics, and what type of content they are most likely to engage with.

This can be done by analyzing your audience's engagement with your content, such as likes, comments, and shares, as well as analyzing your video analytics like views, engagement, and retention rate. Additionally, you can use tools like YouTube Analytics to track the performance of your videos, and to see which ones are getting the most engagement. (Link to this tool later in the action plan toward the end of the book.) For example, if you're finding that your audience is engaging more with videos that are more in-depth and informative, it may be worth producing more of that type of content. On the other hand, if you're finding that your audience is engaging more with videos that are more light-hearted and entertaining, it may be worth producing more of that type of content.

Once you have a good understanding of your audience and the type of content that they engage with, you can start creating content that is tailored to their interests. This can include creating tutorial videos, how-to guides, unboxing videos, reviews, and vlogs. Additionally, you should also consider experimenting with different formats such as live streaming, 360-degree videos, and virtual reality. Each format has its own unique set of strengths and weaknesses, and it's important to choose the format that best aligns with your content and audience. For example, animation videos may be better suited for a younger audience, while vlogs may be more appropriate for an older audience. Depending on your target audience, YouTube's algorithm may favor longer videos or shorter videos, and it's important to consider the length of your videos when planning out your content. While shorter videos may be easier to produce, they may not perform as well in terms of views and engagement, or vice versa. On the other hand, longer videos require more time and resources to produce, but depending on the audience they may actually perform better in terms of views and engagement .

Another important aspect of creating content that resonates with your audience is to ensure that your content is visually appealing. This can include using high-quality equipment, good lighting, and editing your videos to make them look professional. Additionally, you should also consider using subtitles, closed captions and other accessibility features, to make your content more accessible to a wider audience.

In addition to creating content that resonates with your audience, it's also important to keep an eye on the competition. Analyze the content that other creators in your niche are producing, and see what type of content is resonating with their audience. By keeping an eye on the competition, you can get inspiration for new content ideas and stay up-to-date with the latest trends in your niche.

Finally, it bears repeating that it's important to regularly review and evaluate the performance of your content. Use YouTube's analytics to track the performance of your videos and make data-driven decisions about the type of content you should be producing. This will help you to identify the type of content that resonates best with your audience and make adjustments to your content calendar accordingly.

Finally, setting realistic and achievable content creation and upload goals is important for maintaining motivation and keeping your channel on track. This can include setting a specific number of videos you want to upload per week or per month, as well as setting a specific number of views or subscribers you want to achieve within a certain timeframe. It's important to note that the goals you set should be realistic and achievable, and it is not only important to set clear and specific goals that align with your overall channel objectives, but also to regularly evaluate and adjust them as needed.

When setting goals, it's important to start small and gradually increase the frequency and volume of your content as you gain more experience and confidence. Starting small allows you to build momentum and establish a consistent upload schedule, which is critical for building an engaged audience. For example, if you are just starting out, you may want to set a goal of uploading one new video per week, and then gradually increase that to two or three videos per week as you gain more experience and confidence.

Measurable and trackable goals are also essential. Instead of simply setting a goal to "increase audience engagement", you could set a more specific goal such as "increase average engagement on videos by 10% over the next quarter." This makes it easy to track your progress and determine whether you are meeting your goals.

In addition to starting small and setting measurable goals, it's important to be realistic about the time and resources you have available to create and upload content. While it's important to set ambitious goals, it's also important to ensure that you are able to achieve them within your current schedule and budget. For example, if you are working a full-time job and have limited free time, it may not be realistic to set a goal of uploading a new video every day.This means that you should take into account the time it takes to research, write, film, edit, and upload a video. Be sure to also factor in any unforeseen obstacles that may arise, such as equipment issues or personal emergencies. By setting realistic deadlines, you can ensure that you are able to consistently upload high-quality content without feeling overwhelmed.

Another important aspect is to be flexible and open to experimenting with different types of content and upload schedules. Every niche and audience is different, and what works for one creator or niche may not work for another. It's important to be open to trying new things, and adjusting your goals as needed. Experimenting with different formats, features and strategies can help you find the perfect balance for your channel and audience.

Additionally, it's important to be consistent, regular uploads are important for keeping your audience engaged and growing your subscriber base. A consistent upload schedule also helps to establish your channel as a reliable source of content, which can encourage viewers to come back for more. This can be achieved by planning your content in advance, and creating a content calendar that outlines the topics, formats, and release dates for your videos. This will help you stay organized and on schedule, and ensure that you are able to maintain a consistent upload schedule.

In addition, you should also make use of analytics to measure the performance of your content and make data-driven decisions. YouTube provides detailed analytics on a wide range of metrics, such as views, engagement, and demographics. By analyzing this data, you can identify which types of content and upload schedules are resonating with your audience, and make adjustments as needed.

Finally, it's important to remember that growing a YouTube channel takes time and patience; it is not a one-time event, but rather an ongoing process. Successful creators are always looking for ways to improve and innovate, and are constantly seeking out new opportunities to grow and expand their channels. It's normal to experience setbacks and obstacles along the way, but by staying organized, on schedule and being flexible, setting realistic and achievable goals, experimenting with different formats and strategies, and using analytics to make data-driven decisions, you can overcome these challenges and continue to grow your channel.

In conclusion, creating a content plan is an essential step in building a successful YouTube channel. It allows you to stay organized, on schedule and consistent in your uploads. It also allows you to identify the type of content that works best for your audience and niche and set realistic and achievable content creation and upload goals.

Chapter 3: Optimizing your Channel

In order to set your channel up for success, it is important to optimize it in a way that will make it easy for viewers to find and engage with your content. This chapter will cover several key elements of optimizing your channel, including how to set up your channel for success, creating a catchy name, a good description, and a profile picture that represents your brand, creating an attractive and easy to navigate channel layout, and using keywords and tags in your channel's title and description to optimize for SEO.

Customizing your channel art is an important part of setting up your channel for success. YouTube allows you to upload a banner image at the top of your channel, which is called channel art. This is a great opportunity to showcase your brand and entice viewers to subscribe to your channel. You can use the channel art to promote upcoming videos, feature your logo, or showcase a montage of your best work. In addition, you can use your channel art to promote your other social media platforms, website or blog. This will help you to increase your reach and gain more followers.

When creating your channel art, it's important to keep in mind that it will appear differently on various devices. Therefore, it's recommended to make use of YouTube's channel art template, which you can find on their website, to ensure that your art appears correctly on all devices.

When creating your channel art, think about what message you want to convey to your viewers. If you're trying to promote your brand, make sure your logo is prominently displayed. If you're trying to promote upcoming videos, consider using text overlays or call-to-action buttons to entice viewers to click through to your channel. If your channel is focused on a specific niche or topic, make sure that is reflected in your banner image. For example, if you are a cooking channel, you could feature a mouth-watering image of a dish you have made. If you are a travel vlogger, you could showcase a beautiful landscape from one of the places you have visited.

You can also use your channel art to create a consistent visual theme throughout your channel and make sure it is consistent with your overall branding. This can be done by using similar colors, fonts, and imagery in both your channel art, videos, and your video thumbnails. This will help to create a cohesive and professional brand image and make your channel more memorable to viewers. Also, make sure to update your channel art regularly. This will keep your channel looking fresh and will give viewers a reason to come back and visit your channel again. You can also use this opportunity to promote upcoming videos or new content.

Another important aspect of customizing your channel art is to make sure that it is visually appealing. This means that it should be high-resolution and well-designed. It's important to keep in mind that it will appear differently on various devices. YouTube will automatically resize the banner to fit different devices, so a high-resolution image will ensure that it still looks good on all screens, therefore, it's recommended to make use of YouTube's channel art template, which you can find on their website, to ensure that your art appears correctly on all devices. Second, keep in mind the safe area. This is the area of the banner that will not be obscured by the channel name and other elements on the page. To ensure that important elements of your image are not obscured, you can use YouTube's channel art template to guide you in placing your design elements. Avoid using low-quality images or busy backgrounds that may distract from the main message. Instead, opt for a clean and simple design that is easy to read and understand.

Additionally, think about what other features YouTube offers that you can use to enhance your channel. For example, you can create playlists to organize your videos into different categories, making it easier for viewers to find the content they are looking for. You can also create a custom channel trailer, which is a short video that automatically plays for viewers when they first visit your channel. This is a great opportunity to showcase your brand and give viewers a taste of what they can expect from your channel.

Another useful feature is YouTube cards, which are interactive elements that you can add to your videos. They can be used to promote other videos, playlists, or channels, as well as to direct viewers to your website or other external links. This is a great way to cross-promote your content and drive traffic to other areas of your online presence.

Finally, consider using YouTube's live streaming feature. Live streaming allows you to interact with your audience in real-time and can be used to host Q&A sessions, product demonstrations, or other events. This is a great way to build a sense of community around your brand and create a more engaging experience for your viewers.

Overall, by utilizing YouTube's features, you can create a more engaging and interactive experience for your viewers, which can help to drive engagement and increase the number of subscribers to your channel. Additionally, by making use of these features, you'll be able to promote your other content and drive traffic to your website, which will help to increase your overall reach and visibility on the platform.

Creating an attention-grabbing channel name, catchy video titles, a compelling channel description, and a representative profile picture are essential elements in optimizing your YouTube channel. The first things that viewers will see when they come across your channel is your video title, channel name, and profile picture, so these elements are the first impressions that viewers will have of your channel, and they play a crucial role in determining whether or not viewers will decide to subscribe to your channel, and whether or not they decide to stay and explore more. A catchy video title and a good channel name that accurately represents your channel and its content will help to attract viewers and encourage them to subscribe.

Choosing a good YouTube channel name can be a challenging task, but it is essential for building a strong brand and attracting viewers. One important factor to consider is the relevance of the name to your niche and content. A name that accurately reflects your channel's focus and theme will make it easier for viewers to find and remember your channel. Additionally, it's important to choose a name that is easy to spell and pronounce, as well as easy to remember. A good YouTube channel name should be short, catchy, and memorable. Avoid using numbers or special characters, as they can make the name difficult to remember and search for. You should consider using keywords in your title, as this can help your channel show up in search results when people are looking for content related to your niche. It's also a good idea to check the availability of the name on different social media platforms, as well as the domain name, so that you can create a consistent brand across all channels.

When it comes to creating a catchy video title, it's important to keep in mind that the title is often the very first impression that viewers will have of your channel, likely in search results or their recommended video feed. A title that is too generic or bland will not entice viewers to click and watch your video. Instead, focus on creating a title that is both descriptive and attention-grabbing. Use keywords that accurately reflect the content of your video and are likely to be searched by your target audience. Additionally, think about what makes your video stand out from others in your niche, and include that in your title.

Your channel's description is another important element that can help to optimize your channel. A good description should be engaging, informative, and provide a clear summary of what your channel is about. Use keywords that accurately reflect your channel's content and are likely to be searched by your target audience. Your channel's description should also be clear and concise, providing a brief overview of the content your channel will be offering. It should also include a call-to-action, such as asking viewers to subscribe to your channel, to ensure they take the next step.

Having a representative profile picture is crucial for optimizing your channel. A good profile picture is also important for creating a strong first impression. Your profile picture is the first thing that viewers will see when they come across your channel, and it can make a big difference in whether or not they decide to stay and explore more. This is the image that will represent your channel and it should be a clear and high-quality image that is representative of your brand. It is also a good idea to use the same profile picture across all of your social media platforms to help to build a consistent brand identity.

Consider using your logo or a headshot of yourself if you're the face of your brand, or any other image that you feel represents your channel. It's also important to note that YouTube's profile picture size is 800x800 pixels, and it will be resized to 98x98 pixels. So make sure that your profile picture is high quality and looks good even at a small size. This image will be used on all of your videos, so it should be visually appealing and easy to recognize.

Your channel layout is the overall design and layout of your channel, and it plays a crucial role in determining whether or not viewers will engage with your content. Creating an attractive and easy to navigate channel layout is essential for making a good first impression on viewers and encouraging them to stay on your channel. A well-designed layout makes it easy for viewers to find the content they are looking for, increases the likelihood that they will subscribe to your channel, and will also help to create a consistent and professional-looking brand identity.

When designing your channel layout, there are several key elements to consider when creating an attractive and easy to navigate channel layout. First, consider the overall aesthetic of your channel. Your channel should have a consistent look and feel that reflects your brand and the type of content you produce. These include using a consistent color scheme, imagery, and font throughout your channel, organizing your channel into sections that are easy to navigate, and using high-quality images and graphics to help to make your channel more visually appealing. It's important to keep in mind that the layout should look good on all devices, including desktops, laptops, tablets, and smartphones.

Next, think about the organization of your channel. A well-organized channel makes it easy for viewers to find the content they are looking for. This includes having a clear navigation menu that allows viewers to easily access different sections of your channel, such as your videos, playlists, and about page. Additionally, consider using a video thumbnail grid to display your videos in a visually appealing way, making it easy for viewers to find and watch your content.

Another important element to consider is the use of white space. White space is the empty space around elements on your channel, such as text and images. This space is important because it can help to make your channel look clean, uncluttered, and easy to navigate. It also allows the important elements on your channel, such as your videos and call-to-action buttons, to stand out more.

Another element to include in your channel layout is a call-to-action (CTA) button. This is a button that encourages viewers to take a specific action, such as subscribing to your channel, visiting your website, or watching another video. A well-placed CTA button can significantly increase the chances of viewers taking the desired action.

It's also important to consider the use of custom backgrounds. Custom backgrounds can be used to make your channel stand out and give it a unique look. This can include using a background image or color that reflects your brand or the type of content you produce.

In addition, you can use YouTube's built-in features to further customize your channel layout. This includes adding sections to your channel, such as a featured video or a playlist section, which allows you to showcase specific content to your viewers.

Finally, it's important to test your channel layout on different devices to ensure that it looks good and is easy to navigate. This includes testing it on different screen sizes and resolutions, as well as different web browsers. You can also ask friends or family members, or even solicit feedback from your social media groups to give you feedback on your channel layout, and make adjustments as needed.

Using Keywords and Tags in your Channel's Title and Description to Optimize for SEO:

Search engine optimization (SEO) is the process of optimizing your channel's title, description, and content, improving the visibility to help it rank higher in search engine results. This is important because the higher your channel ranks in search engine results, the more likely it is that viewers will find and engage with your content. One of the most important aspects of SEO is the use of keywords and tags, which can help improve the visibility of your YouTube channel in search results.

When it comes to optimizing your YouTube channel for SEO, the first thing to consider is your channel's title. The title of your channel is the first thing that viewers will see when they come across your channel in search results, so it's essential that it accurately represents your brand and includes keywords that are relevant to your niche. For example, if your channel is about cooking, you should include keywords such as "cooking," "recipes," "kitchen," and "food" in your channel title. This will help your channel show up in search results when viewers search for those keywords.

Another important aspect of optimizing your channel for SEO is the use of tags. Tags are keywords or phrases that you can add to your videos to help them show up in search results. When you upload a video to YouTube, you can add tags to it in the "Info & Settings" section. Be sure to include tags that are relevant to your video and your niche. For example, if you upload a video about a recipe for lasagna, you should include tags such as "lasagna," "recipe," "italian food," and "cooking." This will help your video show up in search results when viewers search for those keywords. These keywords and tags should be relevant to your niche and should be used in a way that is natural and easy to read. Additionally, you should also include meta tags in your channel's description to help search engines to better understand the content of your channel.

Another important aspect of optimizing your channel for SEO is the use of a good channel description. Your channel description is a short text that appears below your channel title in search results, so it's important to make it as informative and engaging as possible. The channel description should also include keywords that are relevant to your niche. It should give a brief overview of what your channel is about and what viewers can expect to find on it. For example, if your channel is about cooking, you should include keywords such as "cooking," "recipes," "kitchen," and "food" in your channel description. This will help your channel to continue to rank well in search engine results and will also help to keep your channel's branding consistent.

To improve your YouTube channel's SEO even further, you can also use video descriptions, video titles, and video tags. These elements are also important for SEO and should be used in conjunction with the channel title, tags, and description. Video titles, descriptions, and tags should be optimized in the same way as the channel title and description, including keywords that are relevant to your niche and video. This will help your videos show up in search results when viewers search for those keywords.

In addition to these elements, it's also important to keep in mind that YouTube is owned by Google, therefore you should also take into account Google's SEO best practices. This means that you should also focus on creating quality content that is relevant to your audience, and promoting your channel across other platforms to increase your visibility.

In conclusion, optimizing your YouTube channel for SEO is crucial for building a strong brand identity, driving more traffic to your channel, and making it easy for viewers to find and engage with your content. By using keywords and tags in your channel title, description, and videos to optimize for SEO, designing an attractive and easy to navigate channel layout, as well as creating a good channel layout and a engaging channel description, you will improve your channel's visibility in search results, making it more likely that viewers will find and subscribe to your channel. Additionally, by creating quality content that is relevant to your audience, and promoting your channel across other platforms, you can increase your visibility and drive even more traffic to your channel, setting your channel up even further for success and increase your chances of building a large and engaged audience.

Chapter 4: Investing in Equipment

Creating a YouTube channel requires more than just a passion for a particular subject or hobby. To make your channel stand out and attract a large audience, you will also need to invest in quality equipment. It's important to invest in good quality equipment to ensure that your videos look and sound professional. However, with so many different types of equipment available, it can be overwhelming to know where to start. This chapter will discuss the importance of investing in good equipment, provide recommendations for starting a YouTube channel, and explain how to stay within your budget while still getting the necessary equipment.

A good quality camera and microphone are essential for creating high-quality, professional-looking content that will attract and retain viewers, and will keep your audience engaged. Good equipment can make a huge difference in the quality of your videos, from the lighting and audio to the overall visual aesthetic. Poor quality videos will turn viewers away, which is why it's essential to invest in equipment that will produce clear and crisp images and audio. One of the most important things to consider when investing in equipment is the camera. There are two main types of cameras that YouTubers use: DSLR cameras and mirrorless cameras. DSLR cameras are larger, bulkier cameras that have been popular for many years. They offer great image quality and a wide range of lenses to choose from. Mirrorless cameras, on the other hand, are smaller and more compact, making them more portable. They also offer great image quality and a wide range of lenses, but they're more expensive than DSLR cameras.

When choosing a camera, it's important to consider your budget and what features you need. If you're on a tight budget, a DSLR camera is a great option. If you're willing to spend more, a mirrorless camera may be a better choice. Either way, a high-quality camera will ensure that your videos look professional and polished. Look for a camera that offers 1080p or 4K resolution, as well as manual controls for adjusting things like aperture, shutter speed, and ISO. Additionally, you may want to consider investing in a camera that offers good low-light performance, as this will allow you to shoot in a variety of different lighting conditions. For those just starting out, a good quality point-and-shoot camera or a mirrorless camera can produce great results. Some popular budget options for starting a YouTube channel include the Canon EOS M50 Mark II camera, the Canon Rebel T7i, the The Logitech C922, and the GoPro HERO7 for when portability takes priority. Many cameras have built-in Wi-Fi capabilities too, which makes it easy to upload videos directly to YouTube.

Another important piece of equipment to invest in is a good quality microphone. The built-in microphone on most cameras is often not of the best quality, and can result in poor audio. Poor audio quality can be a major turn-off for viewers, and can make it difficult for them to hear and understand what you're saying. A good microphone will help to ensure that your audio is clear and crisp, and will help to make your videos more enjoyable to watch. Investing in an external microphone will greatly improve the audio quality of your videos. There are a variety of options available, from lavalier/lapel microphones, boom microphones, to condenser microphones and USB microphones, depending on your needs and budget. Lapel/lavalier microphones are great for on-the-go videos as they clip onto your clothing. This type of microphone is small and can be attached to clothing, making it perfect for on-the-go filming or for filming vlogs. Lavalier microphones are also great for capturing audio in noisy environments, as they are designed to filter out background noise. Boom microphones are great for studio settings and provide a more professional look. Additional pieces of equipment to remember if you want a boom microphone are a boom pole and a boom arm. A boom pole can help you to keep the microphone at a distance from the camera and reduce unwanted noise coming from the camera and a boom arm can be used to keep the microphone stable and in place.

USB microphones are a popular option for many creators because they are easy to set up and use. It can be plugged directly into your computer or camera, eliminating the need for additional equipment or complicated wiring. This type of microphone is perfect for creators who are just starting out and don't want to invest in expensive equipment. The condenser microphone is another popular option for YouTube creators. This type of microphone is great for capturing high-quality audio and is ideal for creating videos in a studio setting. Condenser microphones are sensitive and pick up a lot of background noise, so they are best used in a controlled environment where you can eliminate background noise. When choosing a microphone, it's important to consider the environment in which you'll be recording. If you're filming vlogs or talking head videos, a lavalier microphone or a directional shotgun microphone will work well. If you'll be recording in a quiet room, a USB microphone may be the best option. If you'll be recording outside or in a noisy environment, a lapel or boom microphone may be a better choice. If you're filming in a studio or doing voice-overs, a condenser microphone will work better.

Another important piece of audio equipment to consider is a pop filter. A pop filter is a device that attaches to the microphone and helps to reduce "popping" sounds caused by Plosive Consonants (specifically "p", "t", "k", "d", "g" and "b") and "wind" sounds caused by Fricatives (consonants with the characteristic that when they are produced, air escapes in a direct stream making a hissing sound). Pop filters are especially useful if you'll be doing a lot of talking in your videos. Additionally, it's also important to invest in a good set of headphones. Headphones allow you to monitor the audio while you're filming, ensuring that the audio is clear and at the right levels. Without a good set of headphones, it can be difficult to tell if the audio is coming through clearly, and you may end up with videos that have poor audio quality.

Lighting is also key to making your videos look professional and polished. Poor lighting can make your videos look dark, grainy, and unappealing, not to mention unprofessional. Investing in a good lighting kit will help to ensure that your videos are well-lit and look great. There are several types of lighting equipment available, including softbox lights, ring lights, and continuous lights. Softbox lights are great for providing soft, even lighting and are often used in studio settings. Ring lights are great for providing even lighting and are often used for makeup tutorials and close-up shots. Continuous lights are great for providing natural-looking light and are often used for outdoor videos.Even investing in a basic lighting kit, including budget soft boxes or ring lights, can greatly improve the look and feel of your videos.

When choosing lighting equipment, it's important to consider the type of videos you'll be filming and the environment in which you'll be filming. If you'll be filming in a studio, softbox lights may be the best option. If you'll be filming close-up shots or in a small space, ring lights may work better. If you'll be filming outdoors or in a larger space, you may need more powerful lights, such as LED panels. Another important factor to consider when choosing lighting equipment is the color temperature of the lights. The color temperature of light is measured in Kelvins (K) and ranges from warm (around 2000K) to cool (around 6500K). Warm light is best for creating a cozy, intimate atmosphere, while cool light is best for creating a bright, energizing atmosphere. Depending on the type of videos you'll be filming, you may want to invest in lights with adjustable color temperature.

In addition to the above, it's also important to invest in a good quality editing software package. There are many options available, from free programs like iMovie and Windows Movie Maker to more advanced options like Adobe Premiere and Final Cut Pro. A good editing software will allow you to create professional-looking videos, with features like color correction, sound mixing, and special effects.

It's also good to have a good tripod to keep your camera steady while filming. There are several types of tripods available, including table-top tripods, lightweight travel tripods, and heavy-duty tripods. Table-top tripods are great for small cameras and can be used on a flat surface. Lightweight travel tripods are great for on-the-go videos and can be easily carried in a backpack. Heavy-duty tripods are great for professional videographers and can support larger cameras. When choosing a tripod, it's important to consider the type of camera you'll be using and the environment in which you'll be recording. If you'll be recording in a studio, a heavy-duty tripod may be the best option. If you'll be recording on the go, a lightweight travel tripod may be a better choice. This will help to ensure that your videos are not shaky and hard to watch.

In addition to these basic pieces of equipment, you may also want to invest in additional items such as a video editing software, a green screen, or a teleprompter, depending on the type of videos you'll be filming. For example, if you'll be filming a lot of action shots, you may want to invest in a stabilizer or a gimbal. If you'll be filming in different locations, you may want to invest in a portable green screen or a portable backdrop stand. These items can greatly enhance the production value of your videos and make the process of creating content more efficient and streamlined.

When it comes to equipment, it's important to prioritize quality over quantity. While it can be tempting to purchase all the latest and greatest equipment, it's more important to invest in the equipment that will best serve the needs of your channel. Keep in mind that you don't have to invest in the most expensive equipment to get good results. There are many affordable options that can work just as well as more expensive options. The key is to do your research, understand your needs, and invest in equipment that will help you achieve the results you want. While it is important to invest in quality equipment, it's also essential to understand the different types of equipment that are available, and choose the right one for your needs. Additionally, consider your budget and don't be afraid to start with the basics, you can always expand as your channel grows. Consider your budget, the type of content you plan to create, and your own personal preferences, be smart about your purchases and make sure you're getting the most value for your money. For example, if you're planning on filming videos outdoors, you'll need equipment that is weatherproof and durable. Similarly, if you're planning on filming videos in low light, you'll need equipment that can handle low light situations. If you're planning to create vlogs or videos in which you're the primary focus, you'll want to invest in a camera with good autofocus and image stabilization.

Starting a YouTube channel can be expensive, especially with so many options for equipment and setups out there, so it's essential to stay within your budget while still investing in the necessary equipment. There are many affordable options for equipment that can still provide high-quality results. A great way to stay within your budget is to rent equipment or borrow from friends when you need it, instead of buying everything outright. It's also important to keep in mind that investing in expensive equipment doesn't guarantee success on YouTube. The most important thing is to create high-quality, engaging content that resonates with your audience. While good equipment can help you achieve this, it's not the only factor. It's important to find the right balance between investing in the necessary equipment and staying within your budget.

One of the first things to consider when trying to stay within a budget is the type of videos you plan to create. If you'll be filming in a studio and need lighting equipment, softbox lights may be a more affordable option than professional lighting setups. Similarly, if you'll be filming on location, a portable light kit may be more practical and cost-effective than a larger, more expensive setup.

Another way to save money while still investing in necessary equipment is to consider buying used or refurbished equipment. This can be a great way to get high-quality equipment at a fraction of the cost of buying new. However, it's important to do your research and make sure you're buying from a reputable seller, as some used equipment may be in poor condition or not work properly.

Renting equipment is another option to consider if you're on a tight budget. This can be a great way to get access to high-quality equipment without the cost of buying it outright. Many camera and equipment rental companies offer rental packages at a variety of price points, making it easy to find something that fits within your budget.

It's also important to be mindful of your expenses over time. YouTube success doesn't happen overnight and it's important to be prepared for the long term. For example, if you're buying a camera or other piece of equipment, think about the cost of replacement parts and repairs, as well as the cost of any additional equipment you'll need to purchase in the future.

In addition, it's important to consider the cost of other equipment that you may need for your channel such as a good microphone, a tripod, a good laptop or computer, editing software, and any other equipment that is necessary for your channel.

Another way to stay within your budget is to consider the features that you actually need. Do you need a camera with 4K resolution if you're not going to be filming in 4K? Do you need a high-end microphone if your videos are mostly talking-head style? By being mindful of the features you actually need, you can find equipment that fits your budget while still providing the quality you need.

When it comes to starting a YouTube channel, it's important to strike a balance between investing in high-quality equipment and staying within your budget. By being mindful of the type of videos you plan to create, considering used or refurbished equipment, renting equipment, thinking about the cost of replacement parts and repairs, and being mindful of the features you actually need, you can find equipment that fits your budget while still providing the quality you need to create professional-looking videos. A good quality camera, microphone, tripod, and lighting equipment can improve the production value of your videos, help to create a professional-looking video, and ultimately, attract and retain a larger audience, however,, it is important to understand the different types of equipment available, choose the right one for your needs, and stay within your budget while still investing in the necessary equipment.

Chapter 5: Creating Engaging Content

Creating engaging, informative, and entertaining content is one of the most important factors for a successful YouTube channel. In this chapter, we will explore some tips, strategies, and best practices for creating content that will keep your audience interested, entertained, engaged and coming back for more.

The first step in creating engaging content is to understand your target audience and what they want to see. This can be achieved by conducting research and using tools like analytics to understand what kind of content is performing well and what kind of content your audience is responding to. Who are they? What do they like? What do they need? To get a good understanding of your audience, consider conducting surveys, focus groups, or even just asking your existing followers what they enjoy watching and what they'd like to see more of. This information can be used to create a content plan that is tailored to your audience's interests and needs.

The script is the backbone of your video, and it's important to take the time to craft a compelling one. Write a script that is engaging, informative, and entertaining, and that keeps your viewers hooked from start to finish. One of the key aspects of creating engaging and memorable content is by weaving a compelling story throughout the production. Storytelling can help to create an emotional connection with the audience, making them more invested in the content and more likely to remember it. Storytelling is an age-old art that has been used to capture the attention and imagination of audiences for generations, and in the world of video production, storytelling is just as important as it has ever been. Whether you are creating a documentary, a commercial, or a promotional video, storytelling is a key component that can help you keep your audience interested and engaged. Here are a few tips to help you use storytelling and other techniques to keep your audience interested:

Identifying the story: The first step in incorporating storytelling into a video production is to identify the story you want to tell.

This can be a personal story about the experiences of the people involved in the production, a narrative that ties together the different elements of the video, or a story that provides context for the information you're presenting.

Developing the narrative: Once you've identified the story, you need to develop the narrative. This involves breaking down the story into its key components, including the characters, the setting, the conflict, and the resolution. You should also consider the pacing of the story and how you can use visual and audio elements to support the narrative.

Creating a storyboard: A storyboard is a visual representation of the story that you want to tell. It helps you to plan the shots and sequences of the video and to visualize how the story will unfold. This can be as simple as a series of sketches or as complex as a detailed animation.

Filming the video: Once you have a clear understanding of the story you want to tell and a storyboard to guide you, it's time to start filming. When filming, make sure to stay true to the storyboard and keep the audience's perspective in mind. You should also think about how you can use different camera angles, lighting, and sound effects to support the narrative and keep the audience engaged.

Start with a hook: The first few seconds of your video are critical. You need to grab your audience's attention and make them want to keep watching. To do this, start your video with a hook, something that will grab their attention and make them want to know more. This could be a surprising statistic, a dramatic scene, or an attention-grabbing sound effect.

Use strong visuals: Visuals are a powerful way to communicate your story and keep your audience engaged. Make sure your visuals are high quality and relevant to your story. If possible, use a mix of static images, animations, and video footage to create a dynamic and visually interesting experience for your audience.

Create a clear narrative: When it comes to storytelling, a clear narrative is essential. Your story should have a beginning, middle, and end, and it should be easy to follow. Make sure your story has a clear message and that it is told in a logical order.

Use characters: People love to connect with characters, and using characters can help you keep your audience interested in your story. If possible, create a protagonist that your audience can root for and a villain that they can despise. This will help to create a clear narrative and make your story more engaging.

Embrace humor: Humor can be a powerful tool for keeping your audience interested in your story. Whether you're using physical comedy, satire, or irony, puns, jokes, or humorous situations, a bit of humor can go a long way in making your audience feel more invested in your story, or help to lighten the mood and provide a break from the more serious content.

Engaging the audience: Engaging the audience is key to keeping them interested in a video production. This can be achieved through the use of interactive elements, such as quizzes, polls, or challenges, or by asking the audience to participate in the production through social media.

Use sound: Sound is an often-underrated aspect of video production, but it is incredibly important. Make sure you are using sound in a deliberate and effective way. Use music to set the mood and to create an emotional connection with your audience. Use sound effects to enhance your visuals and to create an immersive experience for your audience.

Creating visual interest: Engaging visuals can help to keep an audience interested in a video production. This can be achieved through the use of animation, special effects, or simply by making sure that the shots are visually interesting and well composed.

Create a call to action: At the end of your video, make sure you have a clear call to action. Whether you are asking your audience to share your video, to visit your website, or to make a purchase, make sure your call to action is clear and easy to follow.

Editing the video: The final step in incorporating storytelling into a video production is editing. This is where you bring all of the elements of the story together and refine the pacing, tone, and overall feel of the video.

These are just a few tips for using storytelling and other techniques to keep your audience interested. Remember, the most important thing is to create a story that is engaging, informative, and entertaining. If you can do that, you'll be well on your way to creating a successful video.

In addition to writing a compelling script, it's important to use visual elements to enhance your story and make your content more engaging. This can include adding images, graphics, animations, and engaging narration, as well as incorporating camera shots, transitions, and other visual elements to help convey your message and keep your viewers engaged. Don't be afraid to try new things, experiment and push the boundaries. Your creativity will help set you apart from the competition and make your content more engaging. Your audience wants to learn and grow, so make sure your content is informative and educational. Share your knowledge, experience and insights with your audience, and they'll keep coming back for more. Additionally, using humor, personal anecdotes, and behind-the-scenes footage can also help to keep your audience interested and entertained. Humor is a great way to engage your audience and keep them entertained. Note, when incorporating humor into your content, make absolutely sure it's appropriate for your target audience.

Music and sound effects can add an extra layer of interest and excitement to your videos, making them more engaging and memorable. Choose background music or sound effects that complement your content and help to set the mood and atmosphere. Finally, it's important to encourage interaction and engagement from your viewers. You can do this by asking questions, creating polls, or even holding contests or giveaways. Encouraging interaction will help to build a sense of community around your content and keep your viewers coming back for more.

Creating a content calendar and sticking to a consistent upload schedule are essential components of any successful content creation strategy. A content calendar helps you plan and organize your content in advance, ensuring that your audience always has something new and interesting to look forward to. It also helps you stay on track and avoid gaps in your content schedule. Earlier we covered a lot of ways to create and use your content calendar, but there are also specific tools for content planning, such as Trello or Hootsuite you can integrate as well or even use as stand-alone content calendars. (There will be links to these tools later in the action plan toward the end of the book.) Whichever format you choose, make sure your content calendar is easily accessible and that you have the ability to update it regularly. Having it hosted online so that you can access it from your phone, whether through a browser or an app can be very useful as well.

Another important aspect of creating engaging content is to always be experimenting and testing new formats, features, and strategies to see what works best for your channel. This can be achieved by trying new things and being open to feedback from your audience. Analytics allows you to track the success of your content and make data-driven decisions about what works and what doesn't. This can be achieved by using tools like Google Analytics to track your audience's engagement, retention, and feedback. This information can be used to identify areas of improvement and make changes to your content strategy as needed.This will help you to stay up-to-date with the latest trends and algorithms on YouTube, and ensure that you are always delivering the best possible content for your audience. There are several key metrics that you should pay attention to when measuring the performance of your content. These include:

Views: The number of times your video has been watched. This is a basic but important metric that gives you an idea of how many people are watching your videos.

Watch time: The total amount of time people are spending watching your videos. This metric gives you an idea of how engaged your audience is with your content.

Audience retention: The percentage of viewers who watch your entire video. This metric gives you an idea of how well your content is holding your audience's attention.

Engagement rate: The number of likes, comments, and shares your video receives. This metric gives you an idea of how your audience is interacting with your content and how it is resonating with them.

Traffic source: The sources from which your viewers are coming to your videos. This metric gives you an idea of where your audience is coming from and what channels are driving the most traffic to your videos.

By tracking these metrics, you can gain a better understanding of what is working well with your content and what can be improved. For example, if you see that your audience retention is low, this may indicate that your content is not engaging enough or that it is too long. In this case, you may want to consider making changes to your content or trimming down its length.

It's also important to use analytics to identify trends and patterns in your audience behavior. For example, if you notice that your videos tend to perform better on certain days of the week, you can use this information to schedule your content accordingly. Similarly, if you notice that certain topics are more popular with your audience than others, you can focus on creating more content around these topics. To use analytics effectively, it's important to choose the right analytics tool for your needs. There are many different analytics platforms available, including Google Analytics, YouTube Analytics, VidIQ and TubeBuddy. (There will be links to these tools later in the action plan toward the end of the book.) Each of these platforms offers different features and benefits, so it's important to choose one that best fits your needs. So, if you're serious about creating great video content, be sure to invest in a good analytics platform and start tracking your performance today!

In conclusion, creating engaging content is an ongoing process that requires patience, persistence, and a willingness to experiment and test new things. By understanding your target audience, using storytelling and other techniques, creating a content calendar, using analytics, and experimenting with new formats and features, you will be able to create content that is engaging, entertaining, and relevant for your audience.

Chapter 6: Promoting your Channel

Promoting your YouTube channel is crucial to growing your audience and building your brand. As a YouTube creator, it is important to promote your channel effectively in order to reach a wider audience and grow your subscribers. There are several strategies you can use to promote your channel and build your brand. In this chapter, we will explore some tips and strategies for promoting your channel effectively.

Use Social Media and Other Platforms

Social media platforms such as Twitter, Instagram, TikTok, and Facebook are powerful tools for promoting your channel. You can share your latest videos and updates with your followers, participate in discussions and engage with your audience, and drive traffic to your channel. It's important to post regularly and consistently while utilizing hashtags to increase the visibility of your posts, build a following, and keep your followers engaged and interested in your content. By utilizing the various features available on different social media platforms, you can maximize your reach and engagement with your audience.

Additionally, you can use platforms like Reddit, LinkedIn, and other forums that are relevant to your niche to promote your channel. You can engage in conversations and share your content with like-minded individuals on these external platforms to reach a wider audience. Growing your audience takes time and effort, but there are a few strategies you can use to help speed up the process.

One of the most effective ways to use social media for promoting your channel is to post regular updates and teasers of your content. This allows you to keep your audience engaged and informed about what they can expect from your channel. When posting updates, it is important to choose high-quality images and videos that effectively showcase your content. Make sure to share your videos on your social media accounts along with a catchy caption and relevant hashtags. You can also join relevant groups and engage with other users in your niche to reach more people.

In addition to posting updates and teasers, you can also use social media to interact with your audience. By responding to comments and messages, you can build stronger relationships with your viewers and increase their engagement with your channel. It is also important to engage with other creators and influencers in your niche, as this can lead to potential collaborations and cross-promotion opportunities.

Another way to use social media to promote your channel is through paid advertising. By using paid advertising on platforms such as Facebook, Instagram, and Twitter, you can target a specific audience and increase the visibility of your channel. This can be especially useful for reaching new viewers and growing your audience. Optimizing your videos for search engines will help you reach more viewers who are looking for content similar to yours. To optimize your videos, use relevant keywords in your video titles, descriptions, and tags, and make sure your videos have a clear and concise description that includes the most important information.

When promoting your channel on social media, it is important to keep your branding consistent. This means using the same profile picture, cover photo, and color scheme across all of your social media accounts. This helps to build brand recognition and increase the credibility of your channel. Your video thumbnails are the first thing viewers see when they find your video, and they play a critical role in whether or not they decide to watch. Make sure your video thumbnails are eye-catching, and provide a clear preview of what the video is about. You can use eye-catching images, text, and graphics to create thumbnails that stand out.

In addition to using social media, it is also important to promote your channel on other platforms, such as your blog or website. By including links to your YouTube channel on these platforms, you can drive traffic and increase the visibility of your channel. You can also use email marketing to promote your channel and keep your audience informed about your content.

Collaborate with other creators in your niche: Find creators with similar interests or a complementary niche and reach out to them about collaborating on a video or promoting each other's channels. This can lead to cross-promotion, which is a win-win situation for both creators. When you collaborate with another creator, you can reach their followers, and they can reach yours. Make sure to find creators with a similar target audience, and create content that is relevant and interesting to both of your audiences.

Engage with your audience: Engaging with your audience is key to promoting your channel and building a loyal following. Hosting giveaways and contests is a fun way to engage your audience and encourage them to share your content with their friends and followers. You can encourage viewers to share your videos, leave comments, or subscribe to your channel, and then select a winner from the participants. This is a fun and effective way to grow your audience, and you can also promote your giveaway or contest on social media to reach a wider audience.Responding to comments, answering questions, and responding to feedback shows your audience that you value their opinions and appreciate their support. Respond to comments and messages, ask for feedback, and participate in discussions. This type of engagement can help build a loyal following and increase your reach.

Building Relationships with Other Creators and Influencers

Building relationships with other creators and influencers in your niche can be a highly effective way to expand your reach, introduce your channel to new viewers, and grow your audience. This can be accomplished through a variety of means. You can work together on videos, share each other's content, have guest appearances on other channels, and even just directly support each other's channels. Collaborating with other creators can also help you reach new audiences and gain exposure for your channel. This can lead to cross-promotion, which is a win-win situation for both creators.

One of the easiest ways to start building relationships with other creators in your niche is by reaching out to them. This can be done through social media, email, or even by commenting on their videos. When reaching out to other creators, it's important to be friendly, professional, and respectful. You should also make sure to clearly articulate the value that you can bring to the relationship. For example, you could mention how a collaboration would benefit both of your channels, or how you can help each other grow your audiences. One of the best ways to build relationships with other creators in your niche is by collaborating on content. Collaborations can take many forms, such as creating joint videos, hosting each other's videos on your channels, or even co-hosting a series of videos. Collaborations can be a great way to bring new life to your channel, reach new audiences, and gain new subscribers. When collaborating with other creators, it's important to choose partners who complement your channel and share your values. Sharing and promoting other creators' content is another great way to build relationships and promote your channel. When you share or promote other creators' content, it shows that you support them and value their work. In return, they may be more likely to support you in the future. Additionally, by promoting other creators' content, you can tap into their audience and reach new viewers who may not have discovered your channel otherwise.

Attending industry events and conferences can help you network with other creators and brands. You can also showcase your channel and meet potential collaborators and sponsors. Additionally, attending events can help you stay up-to-date with the latest trends and advancements in the industry. Joining online communities related to your niche is another great way to build relationships with other creators and influencers. These communities can be a great place to connect with other like-minded individuals, share your work, and gain insights into the latest trends and opportunities in your niche. Online communities can also be a great place to network and find potential collaborators or promotional partners. Influencer marketing is also a powerful way to reach a new audience. Find influencers in your niche and reach out to them about promoting your channel. This can be through a shoutout on social media, a collaboration, or a paid sponsorship. Utilizing paid promotion, such as Google AdWords or Facebook Ads, can help you reach a wider audience. (There will be links to these tools later in the action plan toward the end of the book.) Target specific keywords and demographics to reach your desired audience. This can be a useful tool for reaching new subscribers and growing your channel. Your video thumbnails and descriptions also play a crucial role in promoting your channel. Choose eye-catching thumbnails and write engaging descriptions that accurately represent the content of your videos. This can help entice viewers to click and watch your videos.

Creating a Brand for Your Channel

One of the most important elements of growing a successful YouTube channel is creating a strong brand identity. Creating a brand for your channel is essential for building your identity and standing out from the competition in a crowded market. A brand is essentially the image, personality, and message that people associate with your channel. Your brand is what sets you apart from your competition, and it's what makes people recognize and remember your channel. The more memorable and distinctive your brand is, the easier it will be for you to grow your channel and reach your goals.

Your brand should reflect your personality, values, and style. Building a brand for your channel requires a consistent and cohesive approach to your content, messaging, and overall image. You want your brand to be consistent across all platforms and media, so that your audience recognizes you and your message no matter where they encounter you. You can create a brand by developing a consistent look and feel for your channel. This includes things like your logo, profile picture, video content, descriptions, and even your tone of voice, and using the same colors, logos, and fonts in all your videos and promotional materials. Choose a consistent color scheme, font, and imagery to use in all of your promotional materials. Your brand should also reflect your niche and the content you produce. Email marketing your brand can be a very powerful tool for promoting your channel and increasing its lifetime value.

To create a brand for your channel, start by thinking about the overall message that you want to convey. What do you stand for? What is your mission? What makes your channel unique and different from others in your niche? Once you have a clear idea of your brand message, you can start to think about the visual elements of your brand. This may include creating a logo or visual identity that represents your channel and reflects your message.

Consistency is key when it comes to promoting your brand. This means using the same logo, profile picture, and tone of voice across all platforms. You should also use the same brand colors and imagery in your videos and other content. This consistency helps to reinforce your brand identity and makes it easier for people to recognize your channel and remember you.Another important aspect of promoting your brand is being active on social media. This allows you to reach a wider audience and engage with your fans and followers. You should regularly post updates and content on social media platforms like Twitter, Instagram, and Facebook. You can also use social media to promote new videos and interact with your audience.

In addition to social media, you should also consider other platforms and media to promote your brand. This may include your own website, blog, or podcast. You may also want to consider creating merchandise or merchandise drops to promote your brand and make money at the same time. By creating a comprehensive and consistent approach to promoting your brand across all platforms and media, you can increase the visibility and reach of your channel and build a loyal following. Promoting your videos through email is another great way to reach your existing audience and keep them informed of your latest content. You can use an email service provider to create an email list, and then send out regular updates to your subscribers, including links to your latest videos. This can help build a strong relationship with your audience and increase engagement.

Building a brand for your channel is essential for success on YouTube. A strong brand identity helps to set you apart from your competition, makes it easier for people to recognize and remember your channel, and makes it easier for you to grow your audience and reach your goals. By consistently promoting your brand across all platforms and media, you can increase your visibility and reach, and build a loyal following that supports you and your channel.

In conclusion, promoting your channel is a crucial aspect of growing your YouTube channel. Growing your audience on YouTube takes time, effort, and a well-executed strategy. By leveraging social media, collaborating with other YouTubers and influencers, building relationships, optimizing your videos for search engines, engaging with your audience, running giveaways and contests, creating eye-catching thumbnails, and promoting your videos through email, and creating a strong brand, you can reach new audiences, engage with your followers, and grow your channel. With persistence, patience, and hard work, you can achieve your goals and succeed on YouTube.

Chapter 7: Monetizing your Channel

In this chapter, we will explore the different ways in which you can monetize your YouTube channel to make a sustainable income, best practices for making a sustainable income, and how to choose the right monetization option for you. YouTube has become one of the most popular platforms in the world, and many creators have found success in monetizing their channels. While creating content and building an audience can be a rewarding experience in itself, monetizing your channel can provide you with financial stability and help you turn your hobby or passion into a full-time career.

One of the most popular, most common and most accessible ways to monetize a YouTube channel is through ads. AdSense, YouTube's ad revenue sharing program, allows you to make money from ads displayed on your videos. When a viewer clicks on an ad, the creator earns a portion of the revenue generated. To get started with AdSense, you need to be over 18 years old, have a valid YouTube account and an active AdSense account. In addition, you need to have a minimum of 1000 subscribers and 4000 hours of watch time in the past 12 months at the time of application. Once you meet these requirements, you can sign up for the YouTube Partner Program and start earning money from ads on your videos. The amount you earn will depend on the number of views your videos receive, the type of ads displayed, and the country your audience is in.

To maximize your earnings from ads, it's important to have a large and engaged audience. This means creating high-quality and engaging content that will keep viewers coming back for more. It's also important to have a consistent upload schedule, as this will help keep your audience engaged and coming back to your channel. Additionally, making use of keywords, tags, and a strong channel description will help optimize your channel for search engines and increase the chances of your videos being discovered by potential viewers.

Sponsorships and collaborations are also great ways to monetize your channel. This involves partnering with a brand and promoting their products or services in your videos. Brands and businesses are always looking for new ways to reach their target audience, and partnering with popular YouTubers can provide them with that exposure. Sponsorships can take many forms, from product placement in your videos, to creating dedicated videos for the brand. The amount you can earn from sponsorships varies greatly, depending on the size of your audience, the niche you're in, and the type of sponsorship you're offering. To find sponsorships, you can reach out to brands that are related to your niche, or use platforms such as Influencer.co or AspireIQ to find opportunities. (There will be links to these tools later in the action plan toward the end of the book.) It's important to choose sponsorships that align with your brand and values, and to only work with brands that are a good fit for your audience. It's also crucial to be transparent with your audience about the sponsorship, and to make sure that you're only promoting products or services that you believe in and that you would use yourself.

Collaborations are similar, but they involve working with other YouTubers or content creators in your niche to create a video together. This can be in the form of cross-promoting each other's channels, or creating content together. Collaborations are a great way to reach new audiences, grow your channel, and increase your earnings. Collaborating with other creators in your niche can also help you build relationships and gain exposure in the community. To find collaboration opportunities, you can reach out to other creators in your niche and see if they're interested in working together. You can also join online forums or communities for YouTube creators and connect with other creators there. When collaborating, it's important to choose partners who are a good fit for your brand and values, and who have a similar target audience to yours. Both of these options can provide you with a significant source of income, but it is important to ensure that the content you create is of high quality and adds value to your audience.

Another way to monetize your channel is through merchandise. If you have a loyal and engaged following, you can consider selling merchandise such as t-shirts, mugs, or other products with your channel's logo or branding on them. This not only provides you with a source of income, but it also helps you to build your brand and increase your visibility. One way to sell merchandise is by using a print on demand service. These services allow you to create and sell products without having to hold any inventory. All you need to do is design your product and upload the design to the print on demand service. They will handle the printing, shipping, and customer service for you.

Some popular print on demand services include CafePress, Teespring, and Redbubble. (There will be links to these tools later in the action plan toward the end of the book.) These platforms have easy-to-use tools that make it simple to create and sell products with your design. You can customize your product offerings, pricing, and shipping options to suit your needs. When using a print on demand service, it's important to keep in mind that the profit margins can be smaller compared to selling physical products yourself. However, it's a low-risk option for monetizing your channel as you only invest time in designing the products, rather than any upfront costs for manufacturing or storing inventory. With print on demand services, it's easy to get started and can provide you with a steady source of income with minimal to no investment upfront. By offering high-quality products that align with your brand and catering to your target audience, you can increase your visibility and build a loyal following.

Next up, offering premium content or memberships can also be an effective way to monetize your channel. This type of monetization strategy involves providing exclusive access or benefits to your audience in exchange for financial support. For example, you can offer behind-the-scenes content, early access to new videos, or premium tutorials to those who sign up for a monthly or annual subscription. This type of content can incentivize your audience to support you financially and provide you with a stable source of income.

There are various platforms that you can use to offer premium content or memberships to your audience, including Patreon and Kofi. (There will be links to these tools later in the action plan toward the end of the book.) Patreon is a platform that allows creators to receive recurring payments from their supporters or patrons. You can offer different levels of membership to your patrons, each with its own set of benefits and perks. For example, you can offer a basic membership for free, but charge a fee for access to premium content or early access to new videos. Kofi is another platform that allows you to monetize your channel by offering memberships and premium content. Kofi is similar to Patreon, but it is focused on supporting content creators and influencers on platforms like YouTube and Twitch. With Kofi, you can set up memberships, offer perks to your supporters, and receive recurring payments. By offering value to your audience, you can incentivize them to support you financially and grow your channel over time. It's important to choose a monetization strategy that aligns with your goals, values, and audience, and to be transparent about your monetization efforts with your audience.

Using a YouTube channel to drive traffic to a product funnel is a common marketing strategy for businesses and entrepreneurs. A product funnel refers to a series of steps that a potential customer takes to eventually make a purchase. By creating and sharing valuable content on YouTube, you can attract a targeted audience and guide them through your product funnel. To use your YouTube channel to drive traffic to a product funnel, you first need to create content that is relevant and useful to your target audience. This could include tutorials, product demonstrations, or industry insights. The goal of this content is to establish your expertise, build trust with your audience, and demonstrate the value of your products or services.

Once you have established a relationship with your audience, you can start to promote your products or services through your videos. This can be done through subtle product placements, calls to action in your videos, or by including links to your product pages in your video descriptions. Another way to drive traffic to your product funnel from YouTube is by creating landing pages specifically for your YouTube audience. These landing pages can be customized to reflect the interests and needs of your YouTube audience and can include specific offers or discounts for those who come from your YouTube channel. Additionally, you can use YouTube ads to reach a larger audience and drive more traffic to your product funnel.

YouTube ads can be targeted to specific audiences based on demographics, interests, and behaviors, making it easier to reach your target audience and convert them into customers.

Affiliate marketing is a form of monetization where a creator earns a commission for promoting someone else's product. For example, if a creator reviews a product on their YouTube channel and includes an affiliate link in the description, they will earn a commission if someone clicks on the link and makes a purchase. Using a YouTube channel to engage in affiliate marketing can be a great way to monetize your channel and earn additional income. To make the most of affiliate marketing, it's important to choose products that align with your niche and audience. For example, if you run a beauty channel, you could consider promoting beauty products through affiliate links.

Affiliate marketing for Amazon on your YouTube channel works by promoting Amazon products to your audience and earning a commission on any sales made through your unique affiliate link. To start affiliate marketing for Amazon, you must first sign up for the Amazon Associates program, which is the company's affiliate marketing program. (There will be a link to this tool later in the action plan toward the end of the book.) Once you're approved, you'll receive a unique affiliate link to promote Amazon products. To promote Amazon products on your YouTube channel, you can include links to the products in your video descriptions, add product demonstrations or reviews to your videos, or even create product-focused videos where you highlight a particular product and its benefits. It's important to choose products that align with your niche and that your audience is likely to be interested in. Additionally, make sure to disclose your affiliate relationship with Amazon in your videos and always promote products honestly and ethically.

Affiliate marketing for Clickbank on your YouTube channel is similar to affiliate marketing for Amazon, but instead of promoting products from Amazon, you promote products from the Clickbank marketplace. (There will be a link to this tool later in the action plan toward the end of the book.) To get started with Clickbank affiliate marketing, you must sign up for a Clickbank account and choose products to promote. As with Amazon, you can promote these products on your YouTube channel by including links to them in your video descriptions, creating product demonstrations or reviews, or creating product-focused videos. The key to success with Clickbank affiliate marketing is to choose products that align with your niche and to promote them in an ethical and transparent manner.

When engaging in affiliate marketing, it's important to be transparent about your relationships with brands and products. You should disclose that you're using affiliate links in your videos and let your audience know that you receive a commission if they make a purchase through your link. This transparency builds trust with your audience and ensures that your monetization efforts are in compliance with laws and regulations. Another key factor to keep in mind when using a YouTube channel for affiliate marketing is the quality of the products you promote. It's important to remember that your audience trusts you and looks to you for recommendations. By promoting products that you believe in and that provide value to your audience, you can build a strong reputation as a trusted and credible affiliate marketer. You don't want to compromise your reputation by promoting low-quality or unethical products, so be sure to thoroughly research the products you're considering promoting.

It bears repeating that it's very important to be transparent, choose high-quality products, understand your audience, and offer additional value to your audience. To be successful with affiliate marketing, it's also important to understand your audience and what they're looking for. You can use analytics to determine what types of products your audience is interested in and tailor your affiliate marketing efforts accordingly. Additionally, you should consider offering additional value to your audience when promoting products, such as offering tips, tutorials, or additional resources related to the product.

In conclusion, monetizing your channel is an important step in turning your hobby or passion into a full-time career. Choosing the right monetization option for your channel depends on a variety of factors, including your niche, audience size, and personal preferences. By choosing the right monetization methods for your channel and your audience, you can make a sustainable income while continuing to create high-quality content that your audience loves. Whether you choose to monetize through ads, sponsorships, collaborations, merchandise, or premium content, the key is to be transparent, experiment, and find what works best for you and your audience. Your audience should always come first, and you should never compromise the quality of your content or your relationship with your audience for the sake of monetization. It is also important to remember that monetizing your channel takes time and effort. You need to have a large and engaged following to make a significant amount of money, so it is important to be patient and persistent in your efforts. With time, dedication, and the right strategies, you can turn your channel into a sustainable and profitable business.

Chapter 8: Staying Up-to-date and Experimenting

As the digital landscape continues to evolve, it's crucial for YouTube creators to stay up-to-date with the latest trends, algorithms, and changes on the platform. In this chapter, we will explore the importance of staying informed and the value of experimenting with new strategies to keep your channel growing and thriving.

How to stay up-to-date with the latest trends and algorithms on YouTube

YouTube is a constantly evolving platform, and it's essential to stay informed of any changes or updates to the platform to ensure the continued growth and success of your channel. With the platform constantly evolving, it's important to be in the know about the changes that could impact your channel, and to adjust your strategy accordingly. One of the biggest challenges for YouTube creators is staying ahead of the curve when it comes to changes and updates. This can be done by subscribing to the official YouTube Creator blog, which provides updates on new features and best practices for creators. The YouTube Creator Blog is the official blog for creators on YouTube. It is undeniably the best place to get updates on the latest features and changes to the platform, and to stay informed about the trends and best practices for creators. Make sure to check the blog regularly for new posts and updates. Finally, it is important to stay informed about the YouTube policies, as they can impact your channel. Make sure to read the Community Guidelines and the YouTube Partner Program policies regularly, to ensure that your channel is in compliance.

Additionally, following industry influencers, experts, and thought leaders in your niche on social media can also give you valuable insights into the latest trends and changes in the industry. Participating in online forums and communities can also be very helpful. Many websites, such as Social Media Examiner and Hootsuite, offer newsletters that keep you up-to-date with the latest social media news and trends. Subscribe to these newsletters to stay informed about the changes to YouTube and how they may impact your channel. Attending conferences and workshops for creators on YouTube is a great way to stay up-to-date with the latest trends and algorithms. These events bring together experts from the industry and give you the opportunity to learn from the best. Consider attending events such as the YouTube Creator Summit, VidCon, and Playlist Live.

Joining creator communities, such as the YouTube Creator Academy and Creator Hub, can be a great way to stay up-to-date with the latest trends and algorithms on YouTube. You can interact with other creators, ask questions, and learn from their experiences. Make sure to join a community that is focused on your niche and to participate in the discussions regularly. Following key influencers in your niche can be a great way to stay up-to-date with the latest trends and algorithms on YouTube. Look for creators who have been successful on the platform and who consistently produce high-quality content. Follow these creators on social media and subscribe to their channels to stay informed about the latest trends and best practices. Analyzing your competitor channels can be a great way to stay up-to-date with the latest trends and algorithms on YouTube. Look at what your competitors are doing, what type of content they are producing, and how they are promoting their channel. Use this information to adjust your strategy and stay ahead of the competition.

The algorithm that determines which videos are recommended to viewers is constantly evolving, so it's vitally important to keep up-to-date on the latest trends and updates to maximize your visibility and engagement. It's also important to stay up-to-date with the latest trends in your niche and understand the types of content that are resonating with your audience. This information can be gathered through analytics and audience feedback, and it can help you to create content that is relevant and appealing to your viewers.

The importance of experimentation and testing to see what works best for your channel

YouTube is a constantly evolving platform, and what works today may not work tomorrow. That's why it's important to be open to trying new things and experimenting with different strategies to see what resonates with your audience. Experimentation is a crucial part of growing a successful YouTube channel. By testing different formats, features, and strategies, you can discover what works best for your channel and your audience, which can lead to increased engagement, growth, and monetization. This could involve trying new types of content, experimenting with different editing styles, or incorporating new technologies into your videos. For example, you may want to try creating a new type of content, such as a Q&A format or a live stream. You may also want to experiment with different video lengths, filming styles, and editing techniques to see what resonates with your audience.

One of the main benefits of experimentation is that it allows you to stay ahead of the curve. The YouTube platform is constantly evolving, and by experimenting and trying out new things, you can ensure that your channel stays relevant and innovative. This can help you to attract and retain your audience, and it can also lead to new opportunities for monetization.

For example, you can experiment with different types of content, such as vlogs, tutorials, or live streams. You can also test different video formats, such as vertical or square video, and see which format resonates best with your audience. In addition, you can experiment with different lengths of videos, such as shorter, snackable content or longer, in-depth content, and see what works best for your niche.

Another important aspect of experimentation is testing different monetization strategies. For example, you can test different types of ads, such as pre-roll, mid-roll, or post-roll ads, and see which type of ad is the most effective for your channel. You can also test different types of sponsorships and collaborations, and see which types are most successful for your channel. Additionally, you can experiment with different types of merchandise, such as t-shirts, stickers, or digital products, and see which products your audience is most interested in.

It's important to note that experimenting and testing should not be done blindly. You should always have a clear objective in mind when testing and experimenting, and you should measure the results of each experiment. This can be done through the use of analytics, such as YouTube Analytics, Google Analytics, or a third-party analytics tool. By measuring the results of your experiments, you can determine what works best for your channel and make data-driven decisions.

In addition to measuring the results of your experiments, it's also important to seek feedback from your audience. This can be done through the use of surveys, comments, or live streams. By asking your audience for feedback, you can get a better understanding of what they like and what they don't like, which can help you to make better decisions about the direction of your channel.

The key is to keep an open mind and be willing to try new things, even if they feel outside of your comfort zone. However, it's important to approach experimentation and testing with a clear objective and to measure the results of each experiment, so that you can make data-driven decisions. It's important to remember that not all experiments will be successful, but failure is a natural part of the learning and growth process. Learn from your mistakes and keep experimenting until you find the right combination of strategies and techniques that work for your channel.

Keeping an eye on the competition and learning from their successes and mistakes

Keeping an eye on the competition is a crucial aspect of growing and succeeding in any industry, and YouTube is no exception. As a content creator on YouTube, it's important to keep an eye on what other creators in your niche are doing and to learn from their successes and mistakes.

This doesn't mean copying their ideas or content, but rather taking inspiration and finding ways to differentiate yourself and add your own unique spin on things. By analyzing the successes and failures of other creators in your niche, you can more easily learn what works and what doesn't, and you can adapt these strategies to your own channel.

Here are a few key tips for keeping an eye on the competition and learning from their successes and mistakes:

1. Research your competition: Start by researching your competition and identifying the top channels in your niche. Analyze their content, engagement rates, and subscriber numbers to get a better understanding of their strengths and weaknesses. You can also take a look at the type of content they create, the format they use, and the type of equipment they use to create their content.

2. Watch their videos: Start watching the videos of your competition and take note of what works well and what doesn't. Pay attention to their content style, tone, and overall quality. See if there are any areas where you could improve your own content, or if there are any innovative ideas you could borrow from your competition.

3. Analyze their engagement: Take a look at the engagement rates of your competition's videos. See how many views, likes, comments, and shares they receive and compare this to your own engagement rates. Analyze what makes their content engaging and see if there are any elements you can incorporate into your own content.

4. Keep track of their growth: Keep an eye on the growth of your competition and track their subscriber numbers, views, and engagement rates over time. This can give you a good idea of the rate at which they are growing and what they are doing to drive this growth.

5. Learn from their mistakes: Pay attention to any mistakes your competition makes and take note of what not to do. For example, if they made a mistake with a certain type of content or a certain format, make sure you avoid the same mistake in your own content.

By keeping an eye on the competition and learning from their successes and mistakes, you can improve your own channel and reach a wider audience. However, it's important to remember that you should never copy or plagiarize the work of others, as this is both unethical and illegal. Instead, use your competition as a source of inspiration and take what you learn from them to create unique and original content that sets you apart from the rest. It's also a good idea to collaborate with other creators and influencers in your niche. By sharing ideas and best practices, you can learn from one another and grow together. You can also learn from your competitors by analyzing their metrics and engagement rates. This information can give you valuable insights into what is working well for them and what areas you can improve upon in your own channel.

Constantly seeking out new opportunities and experimenting with new formats, features, and strategies

Finally, it's important to continuously be proactive, seeking out new opportunities and experimenting with new formats, features, and strategies in order to grow and succeed on YouTube. It is not enough to simply maintain the status quo, but instead you must constantly strive to evolve and improve your channel in order to stay ahead of the competition and meet the ever-changing demands of your audience. This could include trying out new video formats, features, and strategies, such as 360-degree videos, live streams, or interactive videos, or utilizing new features, such as end screens or annotations. This not only provides a fresh and exciting viewing experience for your audience, but it also allows you to test new ways of engaging and retaining your viewers. It's also important to stay up-to-date on the latest tools, advancements, and resources available to YouTube creators, as these can help you to streamline your workflow and improve the quality of your content. This includes new camera and editing software, new platforms for promoting your content, and emerging trends in social media. By taking advantage of these new tools and resources, you can make sure that your channel remains relevant and cutting-edge.

Additionally, it is important to continually evaluate your current strategies and see what is working and what is not. For instance, if you find that a certain type of content is not resonating with your audience, you may want to consider adjusting your content creation approach or exploring new topics that align with your niche. On the other hand, if you find that a particular promotional strategy is driving significant traffic and engagement, you may want to consider doubling down on that strategy and finding ways to improve and optimize it further.

In order to constantly seek out new opportunities, it is also essential to stay connected with your audience and understand their needs and desires. This can be done through regular feedback sessions, polls, and surveys, as well as by closely monitoring your analytics and engagement metrics. By staying connected with your audience and staying on top of industry trends, you will be well positioned to identify new opportunities for growth and success on YouTube.

In conclusion, staying up-to-date and experimenting with new strategies on YouTube is crucial for growing and thriving as a creator. By being open to new ideas, networking and staying informed of the latest trends and updates, and continuously seeking out new opportunities, you can ensure that your channel stays relevant and engaging for your audience. With hard work, persistence, and a commitment to growth and improvement, you can build a thriving YouTube channel that engages and retains your audience for years to come.

Conclusion

In conclusion, starting and growing a successful YouTube channel is a challenging but rewarding journey that takes time, effort, and persistence. However, the benefits of having a successful channel can be significant, from building a personal brand to monetizing through ads, sponsorships, and collaborations. The conclusion of this ebook serves as a reminder of the key takeaways and tips for creating a thriving channel. The key to success is to have a clear plan, consistently create high-quality content, and stay up-to-date with the latest trends and algorithms. The conclusion will also emphasize the importance of encouragement and persistence in achieving success on the platform.

The ebook provided an overview of the benefits of creating a YouTube channel and how to turn a hobby or passion into a career. It also provided insight on how to define your niche, create a content plan, optimize your channel, invest in equipment, create engaging content, promote your channel, monetize your channel, and stay up-to-date with the latest trends and algorithms on YouTube. A quick summary of the key takeaways from this ebook include:

1. Defining your Niche - The importance of choosing a niche that aligns with your interests and expertise, researching the demand and understanding your target audience, and identifying the competition within your niche.
2. Creating a Content Plan - The benefits of planning out your content in advance, staying consistent and regular with uploads, and using analytics to measure the performance of your content.
3. Optimizing your Channel - The steps for setting up your channel for success, including creating a catchy title, a good description, and a profile picture that represents your brand.
4. Investing in Equipment - The importance of investing in good quality equipment, recommended equipment for starting a YouTube channel, and staying within your budget while still investing in the necessary equipment.

5. Creating Engaging Content - The tips for creating engaging, informative, and entertaining content, using storytelling and other techniques to keep your audience interested, and sticking to a consistent upload schedule.

6. Promoting your Channel - The strategies for using social media and other platforms to promote your channel, growing your audience, building relationships with other creators and influencers in your niche, and creating a brand for your channel.

7. Monetizing your Channel - The different monetization options available, best practices for monetizing your channel and making a sustainable income, and the importance of being transparent about monetization efforts with your audience.

8. Staying Up-to-date and Experimenting - The importance of staying up-to-date with the latest trends and algorithms on YouTube, experimenting and testing to see what works best for your channel, keeping an eye on the competition and learning from their successes and mistakes, and constantly seeking out new opportunities and experimenting with new formats, features, and strategies.

From defining your niche, creating a content plan, optimizing your channel, investing in equipment, creating engaging content, promoting your channel, monetizing your channel, and staying up-to-date and experimenting, the guide covers all the essential aspects of growing a YouTube channel. The key takeaways from the ebook emphasize the importance of patience and persistence in growing a YouTube channel, and you are encouraged to seek out resources, such as forums and communities, to get more tips and advice on growing their channel.

Starting a YouTube channel may seem overwhelming, and daunting, but with the right planning and approach, it can be a rewarding and fulfilling experience. It's important to remember that success takes time and patience. It is important to seek out resources, such as forums and communities, to get more tips and advice on growing your channel. Surround yourself with like-minded individuals who can support and encourage you. Stay motivated and focused on your goals, and remember to enjoy the journey. Consistency is key in creating a successful channel, as is the willingness to experiment and try new things. Don't be afraid to make mistakes, as they can often lead to growth and improvement. To be successful on the platform, it's important to have a clear understanding of your niche, a well-planned content strategy, optimized channel, and engaging content that appeals to your audience. Additionally, promoting your channel, monetizing it, and staying up-to-date with the latest trends and algorithms are all crucial factors in building a successful channel. With a solid plan in place, consistent effort, the right approach, persistence, and a willingness to learn and adapt, anyone can turn their hobby or passion into a successful YouTube channel and thriving career.

In this ebook, we've covered the key takeaways that can help you get started on your YouTube journey, and provide you with the tools to continue growing your channel. Whether you're just starting out, or you're a seasoned creator, there's always room for improvement and growth. Here are a few tips and pieces of encouragement for getting started and continuing to grow your channel.

1. Get started! Don't wait for the perfect moment, just start filming and uploading content. It doesn't have to be perfect, but it's important to get your channel up and running.
2. Stay organized and consistent with your upload schedule. This is crucial for maintaining and growing your audience.
3. Don't be afraid to experiment and try new things. This is the best way to find out what works best for your channel and your audience.
4. Collaborate with other creators and influencers in your niche. This is a great way to grow your audience, learn from others, and have fun while doing it.
5. Be persistent and patient. Building a successful YouTube channel takes time and effort, but with dedication and hard work, you can achieve your goals.

6. Seek out resources and support from forums and communities. There are many resources available to help you grow your channel and overcome any challenges you may face.
7. Remember to have fun! Creating content and building a channel should be enjoyable, so don't get too caught up in the numbers and focus on having a good time.

Starting a YouTube channel is an exciting journey, but it can also be a challenging one. You'll likely encounter setbacks and obstacles along the way, but it's important to keep pushing forward and not give up. Successful YouTubers know that persistence is key to their success. Growing a successful YouTube channel requires a lot of patience and persistence. It can be easy to get discouraged when progress is slow, but it's important to remember that success takes time. They understand that creating a successful channel takes time and effort, and they're willing to put in the work required to reach their goals. Stay committed to your goals and continue to produce quality content, promote your channel, and engage with your audience. Patience is a very important factor in growing a YouTube channel. It takes time to build an audience, create a brand, and establish yourself as an authority in your niche. You can't expect to see results overnight, but if you stay dedicated and consistent, you'll start to see growth over time.

It's important to have realistic expectations when starting a YouTube channel. There will be moments of slow growth and even periods of stagnation, but it's crucial to keep pushing forward and not give up. By continuously creating and uploading quality content, promoting your channel, and engaging with your audience, you'll slowly but surely build a following and reach your goals. Another factor that contributes to the importance of patience and persistence is the constantly evolving landscape of YouTube. The platform is always changing and updating, and what works one day may not work the next. The key is to be patient, adapt to the changes, and continue to experiment with new strategies and formats to see what works best for your channel.

Remember to focus on your niche, create engaging content, and promote your channel, and you'll be on your way to building a thriving channel in no time. The journey to success on YouTube may be long, but the rewards are well worth it. And above all, have fun, stay positive, and keep pushing forward! With patience and persistence, anyone can create a thriving channel and turn their passion into a career. So don't give up, stay focused, and keep pushing forward towards your goals. The world is waiting for your content, so get started today!

In closing, the key to successful YouTube channel growth is patience, persistence, and a willingness to experiment and try new things. The importance of patience and persistence cannot be overstated when it comes to growing a successful YouTube channel. While the journey may be long and challenging, the rewards and satisfaction of having a successful channel make it all worth it in the end. A successful YouTube channel can provide an opportunity to connect with like-minded individuals, create a personal brand, and monetize your passion. Remember to set realistic expectations, be dedicated and consistent in your efforts, and never give up on your dreams of creating a successful YouTube channel. Surround yourself with a supportive community, seek out resources, and stay up-to-date with the latest trends and algorithms.

As a content creator, it's important to be constantly learning and seeking new tips and strategies to improve and grow your channel. There are many different resources available, including forums and communities, that can help you to achieve your goals.

One of the best places to start is online forums and communities dedicated to YouTube content creation. These communities are filled with other content creators who are passionate about their channels and eager to share their knowledge and experiences. They can provide a wealth of information on best practices, tips for success, and lessons learned from past experiences. By engaging with these communities, you can gain valuable insights into the latest trends and algorithms on YouTube, as well as stay up-to-date on new formats, features, and strategies.

Another great resource for growing your YouTube channel is attending conferences and events specifically designed for content creators. These events provide opportunities to network with other creators, learn from industry experts, and get hands-on training in various aspects of content creation and promotion. Attendees can gain valuable insights into the latest trends and best practices, and leave feeling motivated and inspired to grow their channel.

Online courses and tutorials are also a great resource for content creators looking to grow their channel. These courses and tutorials provide step-by-step guidance on various aspects of YouTube content creation, from setting up your channel to creating and promoting your content. They are designed to be accessible to creators at all levels of experience and can help you to take your channel to the next level.

In addition to online resources, you can also seek out local resources such as meetups and workshops. These events provide opportunities to meet and collaborate with other content creators in your area and gain valuable insights into growing your channel. They also provide opportunities to network and build relationships with other creators and industry professionals. By utilizing these resources, you can gain valuable insights and tips for success, and continue to grow and improve your channel over time. So, don't be afraid to seek out new opportunities and engage with others in the YouTube community – your channel will thank you for it.

With the right approach, and these tips in mind, the potential for success is limitless; anyone can turn their passion into a successful and profitable career on YouTube! So, start your journey today and turn your hobby or passion into a career with a YouTube channel.

Action Plan

Here is a detailed checklist for creating a YouTube channel:

1. Define Your Niche
   - Determine your interests and areas of expertise
     i. Brainstorm a list of your passions, hobbies, and areas of knowledge.
     ii. Reflect on what topics you are most confident speaking about and enjoy discussing.
     iii. Consider the current market demand for content in the areas you listed.
     iv. Research what topics are popular on YouTube and which ones have a large following.
     v. Evaluate which topics align with your interests and areas of expertise.
     vi. Prioritize the topics that have a high demand and are within your area of expertise.
     vii. Consider the potential for growth and sustainability in each topic.
     viii. Narrow down your list to 3-5 topics that you are most interested in and knowledgeable about.
     ix. Reflect on your personal brand and how the topics you have chosen align with your values and personality.
     x. Choose your final niche and focus on creating content within this area.
   - Research the demand for your niche
     i. Identify potential niches you are interested in exploring.
     ii. Use Google Keyword Planner to research search volume for keywords related to your niche.
     iii. Analyze the competition in your niche by researching popular YouTube channels, blogs, and websites.

    iv. Use social media platforms to see what content is resonating with your target audience.

    v. Look at trending topics within your niche and assess the potential for creating content around them.

    vi. Consider the potential for monetization within your niche and evaluate the earning potential.

    vii. Use surveys and other market research tools to gather data about the demand for content within your niche.

    viii. Make a decision on your niche based on your research and assessment of the demand for it.

- Identify your target audience

    i. Define your target audience demographic information, such as age, gender, location, education, and income.

    ii. Identify the interests, hobbies, and values of your target audience.

    iii. Determine what type of content your target audience is interested in and actively searches for on YouTube.

    iv. Look at the channels and videos that are popular in your niche to see what types of content and topics are resonating with your target audience.

    v. Consider conducting a survey or focus group with a small group of potential target audience members to get more specific information about their interests and habits.

    vi. Analyze the data you have collected to create a detailed profile of your target audience, including their wants, needs, and behaviors.

    vii. Use this information to inform your content creation and channel strategy, ensuring that your content resonates with your target audience and meets their needs.

- Analyze the competition in your niche

      i.   Make a list of other YouTube channels in your niche

     ii.   Visit each channel and subscribe to keep updated on their content and growth

   iii.   Study their content types, frequency of uploads, audience engagement and growth

   iv.   Analyze their strengths and weaknesses and take note of what makes them unique

     v.   Research the keywords they use in their titles, tags and descriptions

   vi.   Check their video and channel metrics such as views, subscribers, and engagement rates

   vii.   Take note of their monetization strategies and sponsorships

  viii.   Consider their brand image, messaging, and overall presence on social media platforms

   ix.   Study their engagement with their audience through comments, live streams, and other interactions

    x.   Use this information to inform your own strategies and identify opportunities for differentiation.

2. Create a Content Plan
   - Plan out your content in advance
     i. Determine the type of content that aligns with your interests and niche
        1. Create a list of topics that interest you and align with your niche
        2. Research what type of content is most popular in your niche (i.e. tutorials, vlogs, reviews, etc.)
        3. Consider what unique angle you can bring to the table within your niche
     ii. Create a content calendar
        1. Decide on a consistent upload schedule (i.e. once a week, twice a month, etc.)

2. Plan out the type of content you will create and upload for each date on your calendar

3. Schedule in time for planning, filming, and editing each video

iii. Set achievable content creation goals

1. Consider your current schedule and responsibilities

2. Set realistic goals for the number of videos you want to create and upload each month

3. Create a timeline for reaching your goals and regularly reevaluate your progress

iv. Stay organized

1. Use a planner or project management tool to keep track of your content calendar and goals

2. Create a system for storing and organizing your footage, notes, and ideas for future content

3. Set reminders for yourself to stay on track with your content creation schedule.

o Set a schedule for consistent uploads

i. Determine how frequently you want to upload content to your channel

ii. Consider the amount of time you have available to create and upload content

iii. Make a list of the types of content you want to create

iv. Schedule specific times and dates for creating and uploading content

v. Use a calendar or scheduling tool to keep track of your upload schedule

vi. Prioritize creating a backlog of content to ensure consistent uploads even when life gets busy

vii. Consider creating a content calendar to help you plan out your content for the month or quarter ahead.

viii. Strive for a consistent upload schedule, but be flexible and make adjustments if needed.

- Stay organized with a content calendar
    i. Choose a tool for creating a content calendar, such as Google Sheets, Excel, or Trello.

    ii. Determine your content creation and upload goals, and make sure to align them with your schedule.

    iii. Decide on the frequency of uploads and make sure it is consistent.

    iv. Plan out the topics for each video, including the main points you want to cover and any additional information.

    v. Assign deadlines for the creation, editing, and upload of each video.

    vi. Keep track of the performance of each video, including views, engagement, and feedback from your audience.

    vii. Use analytics to make data-driven decisions about your content calendar and adjust accordingly.

    viii. Regularly review and update your content calendar to make sure it stays on track and aligns with your goals.

- Determine the type of content that works best for your audience and niche
    i. Review existing content in your niche and take note of what seems to perform well.

    ii. Identify the topics and formats (e.g. tutorials, reviews, vlogs, etc.) that your target audience seems to be most interested in.

    iii. Consider the type of content that aligns with your strengths, interests and expertise.

      iv. Experiment with different types of content and measure the performance of each through analytics.

      v. Refine your content strategy based on what is working best for your audience.

      vi. Continuously review and adjust your content strategy to ensure it remains effective and relevant.

- Set realistic content creation and upload goals

      i. Brainstorm a list of potential content ideas that align with your interests and expertise.

      ii. Consider your target audience and the type of content they are interested in.

      iii. Prioritize content ideas based on their relevance to your niche and potential for engagement.

      iv. Create a rough outline or plan for each piece of content.

      v. Determine the time and resources needed to create each piece of content.

      vi. Establish a timeline for creating and uploading content.

      vii. Set weekly, monthly, and quarterly content creation and upload goals.

      viii. Regularly reassess and adjust your content creation and upload goals based on your progress and feedback from your audience.

      ix. Stay flexible and open to experimenting with new content formats and topics.

      x. Celebrate milestones and accomplishments to stay motivated and on track with your goals.

3. Optimize Your Channel

- Choose a catchy title for your channel

      i. Brainstorm a list of potential channel titles that reflect your niche and brand.

      ii. Consider the keywords that you want to optimize for in your title.

    iii. Ask friends, family, or trusted colleagues for their opinions on your title choices.

    iv. Refine your title based on feedback and search engine optimization (SEO) considerations.

    v. Make sure your title accurately represents the content and theme of your channel.

    vi. Keep the title short, memorable, and easy to read.

    vii. Check that your title is not already being used by another channel.

    viii. Finalize your title and make sure it is consistent across all of your social media and branding materials.

- Write a comprehensive channel description
  - i. Define the purpose and focus of your channel
  - ii. Highlight your niche and areas of expertise
  - iii. Include keywords related to your niche for better visibility
  - iv. Provide information about the type of content you plan to upload
  - v. Mention any unique qualities or features of your channel
  - vi. Include a call to action, encouraging viewers to subscribe
  - vii. Keep the description concise and engaging
  - viii. Edit and revise the description until it accurately represents your channel and its content.
- Select a profile picture that represents your brand
  - i. Consider your brand image: What kind of image do you want to convey to your audience? A professional headshot, a fun illustration, or something else?
  - ii. Choose an image that is high quality: Your profile picture should be clear and sharp, so make sure you choose an image with good resolution.
  - iii. Consider the size and shape of the image: The profile picture will be displayed as a circle, so

make sure the important parts of the image are within the circular crop.

iv. Use the same image across all platforms: Consistency is key when building your brand, so make sure you use the same profile picture on all your social media platforms.

v. Test the image: Try different images and see which one gets the most engagement and best represents your brand.

vi. Update regularly: As your channel grows, you may want to change your profile picture to better reflect your brand and style.

o Organize your channel layout for easy navigation

i. Determine the main sections you want to include on your channel (e.g. videos, playlists, about section, etc.)

ii. Decide on the organization and placement of each section, making sure it is intuitive and easy to navigate.

iii. Ensure that the main sections are easily accessible from the main channel page.

iv. Consider adding a menu or navigation bar to make it easy for viewers to find what they're looking for.

v. Make sure that the layout is visually appealing, consistent with your brand, and easy to understand.

vi. Consider adding links to important sections or external resources in the header or footer of the page.

vii. Use images, graphics, and other visual elements to enhance the overall appearance of your channel and make it more attractive to viewers.

viii. Test the layout on multiple devices (e.g. desktop, mobile) to ensure it looks good and is easy to navigate on all platforms.

       ix. Get feedback from friends, family, and members of your target audience to see if they find the layout easy to navigate and understand.

       x. Make adjustments and improvements as needed to ensure the best possible user experience for your viewers.

- Use keywords and tags in your channel's title and description to optimize for SEO

       i. Research relevant keywords and tags in your niche.

       ii. Make a list of the most important and relevant keywords and phrases to include in your channel's title and description.

       iii. Choose a concise, memorable, and descriptive title that includes at least one of your most important keywords.

       iv. Write a detailed and informative channel description that accurately represents your brand and includes a few of your most important keywords.

       v. Ensure that your title and description accurately reflect the type of content that you will be producing on your channel.

       vi. Avoid using over-optimized keywords or misleading information in your title and description, as this could hurt your channel's ranking and reputation.

       vii. Regularly review and update your channel's title and description to ensure that they continue to accurately represent your brand and reflect any changes to your niche or content focus.

       viii. Use relevant keywords and phrases in your video titles and descriptions, as well as in your video tags, to further optimize your channel and videos for search engines.

4. Invest in Equipment

- Determine the equipment you need
  - i. Make a list of the type of content you want to create (e.g. vlogs, tutorials, reviews, etc.)
  - ii. Research the equipment required for each type of content
  - iii. Prioritize the equipment based on importance and budget
  - iv. Invest in good quality equipment that meets your needs and budget
  - v. Make a list of any additional accessories you may need (e.g. tripods, lighting, microphones, etc.)
  - vi. Consider purchasing backup equipment in case of malfunctions
  - vii. Stay up-to-date on the latest equipment and technology advancements in your niche.
- Research different types of equipment and choose the right equipment for your needs
  - i. Make a list of the types of equipment you might need for your content (e.g. camera, microphone, lighting, tripod)
  - ii. Research different types of equipment that meet your needs and budget, such as:
    1. Cameras
       a. action cameras
       b. mirrorless cameras
       c. digital SLRs
       d. Lenses
       e. Tripods
    2. Lighting equipment
    3. Audio equipment
       a. microphones
       b. audio recorders
    4. Video editing software
  - iii. Consider your budget and the level of quality you want to achieve when making your decisions

  iv. Read reviews and watch comparison videos to help you make informed decisions

  v. Take note of the pros and cons of each piece of equipment you are considering

  vi. Choose the equipment that best fits your needs and budget

  vii. Consider purchasing additional equipment to enhance the quality of your content (e.g.

    1. Stabilizer

    2. Lavalier microphone

    3. Green screen

    4. Teleprompter

  viii. Keep in mind that you can always upgrade your equipment later on as your channel grows.

  ix. Test the equipment to ensure it meets your standards and can effectively help you create the content you desire.

 ○ Stay within your budget while investing in quality equipment

  i. Determine your budget for equipment

  ii. Make a list of essential equipment items needed for your type of content

  iii. Research different options for each item and compare prices

  iv. Look for discounts, sales, or refurbished equipment options to save money

  v. Consider the durability, reliability, and compatibility of the equipment

  vi. Read reviews and check for compatibility with other equipment you already own

  vii. Consider any additional costs such as accessories, warranties, or maintenance costs

  viii. Make a final decision and purchase the equipment that best fits your budget and needs.

5. Create Engaging Content

- ○ Use storytelling and other techniques to keep your audience interested
    - i. Identify your story: What is the overall story you want to tell through your channel? This can be the story of your journey, a specific project, or a series of related topics.
    - ii. Get to know your audience: Research your target audience to understand their interests, values, and pain points. Use this information to shape your storytelling.
    - iii. Use attention-grabbing hooks: Start each video with an attention-grabbing hook that draws viewers in and keeps them engaged. This could be a surprising fact, a personal anecdote, or a question.
    - iv. Use visuals: Utilize visuals such as images, graphs, and infographics to support your storytelling and help keep your audience interested.
    - v. Use humor: Humor can be a great way to engage your audience and add levity to your content. But make sure the humor is appropriate for your niche and target audience.
    - vi. Utilize music and sound effects: Adding music and sound effects can help build suspense, create a mood, and support your storytelling.
    - vii. Use transition effects: Transitions can help smooth the flow of your videos and keep your audience interested. Experiment with different transition effects to see what works best for your content.
    - viii. Use different video styles: Try different video styles, such as vlogging, animation, or time-lapse, to keep your content fresh and engaging.
    - ix. End with a call to action: End each video with a call to action that encourages viewers to engage with your content and follow your channel. This

could be a question, a request for feedback, or a preview of upcoming content.

- ○ Consistently upload content according to your content calendar
  - i. Make sure you have enough content ideas to keep up with your schedule
  - ii. Ensure that you have the necessary resources and time to create each piece of content
  - iii. Plan and schedule your content ahead of time using your content calendar
  - iv. Stick to your schedule and upload new content on the designated days and times
  - v. Use a timer or reminder system to keep yourself accountable to your upload schedule
  - vi. Take into consideration any major events or holidays that might affect your upload schedule
  - vii. Continuously evaluate and adjust your schedule as needed to ensure it works best for your audience and content creation process.
- ○ Use analytics to measure the performance of your content and make data-driven decisions
  - i. Set up analytics tracking: Ensure that your YouTube channel is connected to Google Analytics to track and measure your audience's behavior.
  - ii. Identify important metrics: Familiarize yourself with key metrics like views, watch time, click-through rate, subscribers, and engagement rates.
  - iii. Use the YouTube Analytics dashboard: Utilize the YouTube Analytics dashboard to get an overview of your channel performance, including the average watch time, views, and engagement rates.
  - iv. Track your audience's behavior: Use analytics to track how your audience is engaging with your content, such as which videos are being watched,

what type of content is resonating with them, and where they are coming from.

   v. Analyze audience demographics: Use analytics to gain insights into your audience's demographics, such as age, gender, location, and interests.

   vi. Monitor and compare performance over time: Regularly monitor your analytics to compare performance over time and identify trends in audience behavior.

   vii. Make data-driven decisions: Use the insights gained from your analytics to make informed decisions about what content to create, how to optimize your channel, and how to improve your audience engagement.

   viii. Test and iterate: Use analytics to track the results of any changes you make to your channel, and continue testing and iterating based on your results.

6. Promote Your Channel
   - Utilize social media to promote your channel

   i. Create profiles on popular social media platforms (e.g. Twitter, Instagram, Facebook, etc.)

   ii. Make sure your profiles align with your channel's overall branding and aesthetic

   iii. Share links to your videos on your social media profiles

   iv. Engage with your followers by responding to comments and messages

   v. Collaborate with other creators or brands in your niche to reach a wider audience

   vi. Utilize social media ads to target specific demographics and drive traffic to your channel

   vii. Share behind-the-scenes content and teasers to build anticipation for new videos

   viii. Utilize hashtags and keywords to optimize your posts for discoverability

   ix. Utilize social media analytics to track engagement and adjust your strategy accordingly

   x. Consistently post and engage with your followers to maintain a strong presence on social media.

- Connect with other creators and influencers in your niche
  - i. Research and compile a list of relevant creators and influencers in your niche.
  - ii. Follow their social media accounts and engage with their content.
  - iii. Reach out to them through social media or email to introduce yourself and your channel.
  - iv. Offer to collaborate or cross-promote each other's content.
  - v. Attend events or meetups in your niche to network with other creators and influencers.
  - vi. Participate in online communities and forums related to your niche.
  - vii. Join online groups or networks specifically for creators and influencers.
  - viii. Keep track of your interactions with other creators and influencers in a spreadsheet or other tracking system.
  - ix. Continuously cultivate relationships with other creators and influencers to build your network.
  - x. Leverage your connections to gain insights, advice, and opportunities for growth.

- Build relationships with your audience
  - i. Respond to comments on your videos in a timely and personal manner
  - ii. Ask for feedback from your audience and act on their suggestions
  - iii. Collaborate with your audience by asking for their input on future content ideas
  - iv. Engage with your audience by asking questions and starting discussions in the comments

  v. Create a sense of community by hosting live streams and Q&A sessions

  vi. Share behind-the-scenes content to give your audience a more personal look at your life and work

  vii. Provide value to your audience through exclusive content, promotions, or early access to new videos

  viii. Show appreciation for your audience by acknowledging their support in your videos and on social media

  ix. Foster a sense of belonging by creating a branded hashtag or community space for your viewers

  x. Continuously seek out new ways to connect and engage with your audience.

- Create a consistent brand for your channel

  i. Define your brand values and mission

  ii. Choose a color palette and font style

  iii. Develop a consistent tone of voice for all communications

  iv. Establish a consistent posting schedule

  v. Use the same profile picture, logo and channel banner across all social media platforms

  vi. Develop a style guide for all visual elements

  vii. Create branded intros and outros for videos

  viii. Use the same logo and branding in all videos

  ix. Maintain a consistent aesthetic for all content

  x. Use the same hashtags across all social media platforms

  xi. Respond to comments in a way that aligns with your brand voice.

7. Monetize Your Channel

- Determine the monetization options that are right for you

  i. Research different monetization options available on YouTube, such as:

    1. Ad revenue through Google AdSense

    2. Affiliate marketing

    3. Product placements and sponsored content

    4. Merchandising and selling merchandise

    5. Crowdfunding through platforms like Patreon

ii. Decide on the monetization options that align with your goals and values

iii. Determine your niche and target audience to see what monetization options would be most suitable and relevant to them.

iv. Consider the time, resources, and effort required for each option, and how it fits with your content creation and upload schedule.

v. Review the policies and guidelines set by YouTube for monetization options, such as the requirement for a certain number of subscribers or watch hours before you can monetize your channel.

vi. Apply to the YouTube Partner Program to enable monetization on your channel

vii. Enable ad monetization and sign up for Google AdSense

viii. Consider how the different monetization options align with your brand and values, and how they may impact your relationship with your audience.

ix. Consider applying for sponsorships from brands in your niche

x. Look for collaboration opportunities with other creators and influencers in your niche

xi. Consider creating and selling your own merchandise through your channel

xii. Take the time to weigh the pros and cons of each option before making a final decision.

xiii. Plan and implement your chosen monetization strategy.

xiv. Utilize analytics to track your earnings and monitor the effectiveness of your monetization efforts.

xv. Stay up-to-date on any changes or updates in monetization options and regulations, and adapt your strategy accordingly.

- o Stay transparent with your audience about monetization efforts

  i. Clearly disclose any sponsored content in your videos

  ii. Be transparent about any affiliate marketing links in your description or videos

  iii. Be open and honest with your audience about your monetization efforts and how it affects the content you create

  iv. Abide by all applicable laws and regulations, such as disclosing sponsored content according to the FTC guidelines

  v. Continuously evaluate your monetization methods and ensure they align with your values and the expectations of your audience.

- o Follow best practices for monetizing your channel

  i. Research YouTube's policy on monetization and make sure your channel is eligible

  ii. Familiarize yourself with the different monetization options available on YouTube (ads, sponsorships, collaborations, merchandise, etc.)

  iii. Determine which monetization options align with your channel's niche and target audience

  iv. Consider the level of effort and resources required for each option

  v. Make a plan for incorporating monetization into your content creation and upload schedule

  vi. Stay transparent with your audience about any sponsored content or product placements

      vii. Make sure all monetization efforts follow YouTube's guidelines and best practices

      viii. Consider seeking the advice of a professional or seeking out resources to help you monetize effectively.

8. Stay Up-to-Date and Experiment

- Stay informed about the latest trends and algorithms on YouTube
    i. Subscribe to industry-related newsletters or blogs.
    ii. Follow relevant social media accounts and influencers in the YouTube community.
    iii. Attend webinars or online events related to YouTube and video content creation.
    iv. Join online forums or discussion groups for YouTube creators.
    v. Read articles and watch videos about the latest changes to the YouTube algorithm and best practices for success on the platform.
    vi. Regularly check the YouTube Creator Blog for updates and information.
    vii. Stay up-to-date with changes to YouTube's terms of service and community guidelines.
    viii. Utilize resources such as podcasts and books about YouTube success.
    ix. Attend in-person events and conferences for YouTube creators and content creators.
    x. Seek out mentors or experienced creators in your niche for advice and guidance.
- Experiment with new formats, features, and strategies
    i. Brainstorm new content formats to try, such as live streams, Q&A sessions, or vlogs
    ii. Stay up-to-date with the latest YouTube features and tools available to content creators
    iii. Research and try new strategies for audience engagement, such as using calls-to-action or interactive elements

iv. Monitor the performance of your new formats and strategies, and adjust as needed based on the data and feedback from your audience

v. Consider seeking advice from more experienced creators or industry experts to help guide your experimentation efforts

vi. Stay open-minded and willing to take risks, while also being mindful of your brand and values.

- Keep an eye on the competition and learn from their successes and mistakes

  i. Regularly check out competitors' channels

  ii. Analyze the type of content they upload and how often

  iii. Study their engagement levels with viewers (comments, likes, shares, etc.)

  iv. Look into their monetization methods

  v. Identify their strengths and weaknesses

  vi. Consider what you can do differently or better

  vii. Keep track of their growth and success

  viii. Take notes on what they are doing right or wrong

  ix. Stay up to date on the latest industry news and changes

  x. Regularly reassess and adjust your strategy based on your competitor analysis.

9. Seek out resources and advice:
   - Seek out new opportunities for growth and improvement

     i. Identify areas for improvement in your channel and content.

     ii. Research new trends, formats, and features in your niche.

     iii. Analyze the competition to see what is working for them and what opportunities they are taking advantage of.

     iv. Brainstorm new ideas for content and channel growth.

      v.   Attend events, workshops, and conferences related to YouTube and content creation.

     vi.   Connect with other creators and influencers to learn from their experiences and perspectives.

   vii.   Join online communities and forums to stay informed about the latest trends and best practices.

  viii.   Continuously assess your channel's performance and adapt your strategies as needed.

     ix.   Seek feedback from your audience and other industry professionals.

      x.   Take calculated risks and experiment with new strategies to drive growth and improvement.

- Join forums and communities to get tips and advice on growing your channel

      i.   Search for online forums and communities related to YouTube content creation and growth.

     ii.   Identify the most active and helpful forums and communities.

    iii.   Join the forums and communities as a member.

    iv.   Participate in discussions and ask for advice from experienced content creators.

     v.   Take note of the tips and advice given by experienced content creators.

     vi.   Use the tips and advice to improve your channel and grow your audience.

   vii.   Share your own experiences and tips with other members of the forums and communities.

  viii.   Stay active in the forums and communities and continue to learn from others.

     ix.   Consider collaborating with other content creators in the forums and communities.

      x.   Stay up-to-date on the latest trends and best practices in YouTube content creation and growth by regularly visiting the forums and communities.

- Be patient and persistent in growing your channel

i. Remember that building a successful YouTube channel takes time and effort

ii. Stay committed to your goals and vision for your channel

iii. Keep pushing forward, even if you experience setbacks or challenges

iv. Celebrate your milestones and accomplishments, no matter how small they may be

v. Keep learning and experimenting with new strategies and techniques

vi. Stay focused on delivering quality content that your audience will love

vii. Embrace the ups and downs of channel growth and use them as opportunities to learn and grow

viii. Surround yourself with positive influences and people who support your channel and your journey

ix. Stay motivated by setting achievable short-term and long-term goals for your channel

x. Stay true to yourself and your brand, and always be authentic and transparent with your audience.

By following these steps, you can create a successful and growing YouTube channel. Good luck!

Links to Resources

(Note: These links and tool availability may be subject to change. If any links are broken, please send me a message on the Mastery Media website linked below in Appendix A, and they will be updated in the hosted ebook as quickly as possible!)

Niche Research

Google Trends	Google Trends is a useful search trends feature that shows how frequently a given search term is entered into Google's search engine relative to the site's total search volume over a given period of time.	https://g.co/kgs/FgA5Y5
Youtube Search Bar	Use search bar autocomplete for niche ideas	https://youtube.com
Social Blade	Social Blade compiles data from YouTube, Twitter, Twitch, Daily Motion, Mixer, and Instagram and uses the data to make statistical graphs and charts that track progress and growth.	https://socialblade.com
AnswerThePublic	AnswerThePublic listens into autocomplete data from search engines like Google then quickly cranks out every useful phrase and question	https://answerthepublic.com

	people are asking around your keyword.	
SparkToro	SparkToro is an audience research tool that shows the websites your customers visit, social accounts they follow, hashtags they use, and more.	https://sparktoro.com
Google Surveys	Google Surveys is a market research platform that surveys internet users.	https://surveys.google.com
Typeform	Typeform makes collecting and sharing information comfortable and conversational. It's a web-based platform you can use to create anything from surveys to apps, without needing to write a single line of code.	https://www.typeform.com

Keyword Research

Youtube Keyword Planner	The YouTube Keyword Tool enables you to research keywords relevant to your niche and decide on which ones you should focus on based on how many times they are being searched for each month.	https://tuberanker.com/youtube-keyword-tool

vidIQ	vidIQ is designed to boost your YouTube views. Get insight & guidance to grow your channel. Get started for free	https://vidiq.com
TubeBuddy (Very Popular ⊡)	TubeBuddy is a browser extension (aka browser plugin) that adds a layer of very comprehensive tools directly on top of YouTube's website. So many tools...	https://www.tubebuddy.com
SEMRush	SERP tracker, site health checker, traffic analytics, backlink checker, ad analysis & more. 50+ marketing tools	https://www.semrush.com
Ahrefs	Ahrefs is an all-in-one SEO toolset for growing search traffic and optimizing websites. To do that, Ahrefs crawls the web, stores tons of data and makes it accessible via a simple user interface.	https://ahrefs.com
Keywordtool.io	Keywordtool.io is a web-based keyword research and marketing tool that uses the Google Autocomplete feature to generate keyword suggestions for you.	https://keywordtool.io

Keyword Keg	Keyword Keg is a robust and intuitive keyword research suite from Axeman Tech, the makers of the popular Keyword Everywhere browser plug-in. It's suitable for everyone from freelancers to an SEO agency.	https://keywordkeg.com
Keyword Tool Dominator	Save countless hours on keyword research by quickly finding keywords on the most popular search engines and e-commerce marketplaces. KTD's free keyword tools are available for Amazon, Bing, eBay, Etsy, Google, Google Shopping, Walmart, and YouTube.	https://www.keywordtooldo minator.com
Keywords Everywhere	Keywords Everywhere is a freemium chrome extension that helps you with Keyword Research. It shows you monthly search volume, CPC, competition & 12 month trend data on 10+ websites. It also provides traffic, link metrics and back link data.	https://keywordseverywhere .com/start.html
Kparser	What is Kparser? Kparser is a professional keyword research tool that gives	https://kparser.com

	thousands of long tail suggestions from Google, Bing, YouTube, eBay, Amazon.	
HyperSugge st	HyperSuggest is a keyword tool that delivers thousands of keywords and ideas from 9 different networks like Google, Amazon, eBay, Instagram, etc. in seconds.	https://www.hypersuggest.com
Google Trends	Google Trends is a useful search trends feature that shows how frequently a given search term is entered into Google's search engine relative to the site's total search volume over a given period of time.	https://g.co/kgs/FgA5Y5
Google Keyword Planner	You can use this free tool to discover new keywords related to your business and see estimates of the searches they receive and the cost to target them.	https://ads.google.com/home/tools/keyword-planner/
BuzzSumo	BuzzSumo is a tool that helps you discover the best engagement, content and outreach opportunities across social and search.	https://buzzsumo.com

Content Planning

Google Docs/Sheets/ Calendar	A suite of collaborative productivity apps that offers your business professional email, shared calendars, online document editing and storage, and much more.	https://docs.google.com https://sheets.google.com https://calendar.google.com https://drive.google.com
Physical Content Planner	Physical book from Amazon.com	https://a.co/d/jgdfQeu
Trello	Trello is the visual tool that empowers your team to manage any type of project, workflow, or task tracking.	https://trello.com
Monday	An all-in-one work management platform that helps teams streamline their workflow, collaborate seamlessly, and manage complex projects effectively.	https://monday.com
Asana	Asana's web and mobile apps help you stay on track, keep projects organized, and hit deadlines. See project progress, track individual tasks, plan sprints, integrate with other tools, and achieve successful launches.	https://asana.com

Kontent.ai	Kontent.ai is the modular content platform that enables content and engineering teams to create, organize, and reuse valuable content, making every experience consistent and relevant.	https://kontent.ai
DYNO Mapper	Enables users to organize website projects using visual sitemaps, content inventory, content audit, content planning, daily keyword tracking, and website accessibility testing.	https://dynomapper.com
Content Snare	Content Snare is the simple way to collect content & documents from clients. Used by digital agencies, accountants, financial services, lawyers & more.	https://contentsnare.com
Concured	AI Driven tool built to help content marketers better understand the interests of their audience so that they can deliver impactful content that educates, inspires, and resonates.	https://concured.com
Gather Content	A Content Operations Platform, helping thousands of organizations around the world to create quality content, in less time, and at scale.	https://gathercontent.com
HubSpot	HubSpot is a CRM platform with	https://www.hubspot.

	all the software, integrations, and resources you need to connect marketing, sales, content management, and customer service.	com
Basecamp	The easiest place for everyone in every role to put the stuff, work on the stuff, discuss the stuff, decide on the stuff, and deliver the stuff that makes up every project.	https://basecamp.com

Social Media Management

Hootsuite	Social media management software that helps you create content and get more followers. Manage & Schedule Posts To FB, Instagram, LI, Twitter & More.	https://www.hootsuite.com
Brandwatch	Access the world's largest archive of consumer opinion and leverage industry-leading AI to discover new trends before anyone else and make smarter decisions.	https://www.brandwatch.com
Sendible	We're building the tools you need to plan, source, and schedule engaging content seamlessly while helping you reach your social media	https://www.sendible.com

	goals.	
Loomly	An easy-to-use Social Media Management platform that empowers you to craft, optimize, schedule and analyze posts all in one place.	https://www.loomly.com
Content Scheduler (formerly ContentCal)	ContentCal is now known as Content Scheduler in Adobe Express, where you can find social media features alongside thousands of beautiful templates for quickly and easily making and sharing standout content.	https://www.contentcal.com https://www.adobe.com/express
CoSchedule	CoSchedule makes it easier to publish blog posts consistently, schedule social media posts, and drive traffic to your site – all in one tool.	https://coschedule.com
MarketMuse	Cloud-based enterprise content planning solution that helps content marketers, content creators, marketing agencies, publishers and e-commerce companies maximize the value of their online content.	https://www.marketmuse.com
Wistia	Wistia is designed exclusively to support the needs of B2B	https://wistia.com

	companies using video for marketing, support, and sales.	
Canva	Not only can you use it to spice up your social media content, but you can also use it to design things like presentations, invitations, posters, brochures, business cards, etc.	https://www.canva.com

Search engine optimization (SEO) tools

TubeBuddy (Very Popular ⏹)	TubeBuddy is a browser extension (aka browser plugin) that adds a layer of very comprehensive tools directly on top of YouTube's website. So many tools...	https://www.tubebuddy.com
VidIQ	vidIQ is designed to boost your YouTube views. Get insight & guidance to grow your channel. Get started for free	https://vidiq.com
Rival IQ	Social media marketing analytics with advanced competitive analysis, SEO, social reporting and content marketing tools.	https://www.rivaliq.com
YouTube Analytics	YouTube Analytics in advanced mode lets you see more specific data about your channels,	https://studio.youtube.com Log in to your

	assets, and audience. You can also compare content performance metrics and export your data.	youtube channel, then click "Analytics"
Google Keyword Planner	You can use this free tool to discover new keywords related to your business and see estimates of the searches they receive and the cost to target them.	https://ads.google.com/home/tools/keyword-planner/

Paid Advertisements

Google Ads	Google's online advertising program.	https://ads.google.com
YouTube Ads	Choose who you want to see your video ads based on location, interests, and more.	https://www.youtube.com/intl/en_us/ads/
Facebook Ads	Ads across Facebook, Messenger, Instagram or Meta Audience Network	https://www.facebook.com/business/tools/ads-manager
Instagram Ads	With Instagram ads, businesses can drive awareness and increase its customer base through visuals.	https://business.instagram.com/advertising
TikTok Ads	Video ads are available for TikTok itself or for the TikTok family of news apps. They run as 5-60 second full-screen videos in the user's For You	https://ads.tiktok.com/i18n/home

	feed.	
Twitter Ads	Twitter Ads serve to users by competing in an auction. You get to decide how much you pay for each billable action.	https://ads.twitter.com
Pinterest Ads	There's a Pinterest ad format for every one of your business goals. See your options to start boosting awareness, driving sales and increasing conversions.	https://ads.pinterest.com
LinkedIn Ads	Use LinkedIn self-service ads to reach more than 850+ million users worldwide. Build effective ads that target your audience with helpful formats & budget	https://business.linkedin.com/marketing-solutions/ads
Snapchat Ads	Snapchat Ads are designed to help you get the results that are important to you. We'll guide you, but you always remain in control of how much you spend.	https://forbusiness.snapchat.com/en-US/
WhatsApp ads	Businesses can create an ad that clicks to WhatsApp directly from the WhatsApp Business App in the catalog section of the WhatsApp Business app.	https://business.whatsapp.com/products/ads-that-click-to-whatsapp

Sponsorships

Influence.co	Influence.co is the largest community of real humans in the influencer economy. We work with 170k+ influencers, 35k+ brands, and 10k+ agencies.	https://influence.co
Influencer.co	Influencers, managers and agencies can easily tap into social networking audiences to make money, generate tracking links and build reports.	https://influencer.co
AspireIQ	Helps influencers score sponsorships, endorsements, and collaboration deals.	https://aspire.io
Upfluence	Cloud-based influencer management solution designed to help businesses of all sizes manage their social media marketing campaigns.	https://www.upfluence.com
Captiv8	Captiv8 is a great one-stop-shop for all things influencer related!	https://captiv8.io

Walmart Creator	Essentially a new affiliate program that also comes with the opportunity to get free products from the retailer.	https://www.walmartcreator.com
Popular Pays	Platform for collaborating with creators and influencers. Connect, collaborate, and track your performance all in one place.	https://popularpays.com
TRIBE	Influencer marketplace, designed specifically for variety and scale.	https://www.tribedynamics.com
NeoReach	SaaS platform enabling brands and agencies to build their own influencer network and streamline their influencer programs.	https://neoreach.com
#paid	Use #paid to match with brands and create authentic content your audience will love	https://hashtagpaid.com
LTK (Formerly RewardStyle)	RewardStyle/LTK is a fashion, beauty, and home decor affiliate network for bloggers, YouTubers, content	https://company.shopltk.com

	creators, and Instagram influencers.	
Jellysmack	Jellysmack helps creators grow their communities and maximize their earnings across multiple social media platforms.	https://jellysmack.com
Pillar	Pillar is a no-code creator business platform that helps creators to achieve their income goals.	https://pillar.io
Amazon Influencer Program	The Amazon Influencer Program is an extension of the Amazon Associates (affiliate) program, that brings product-related content from Influencers onto Amazon.	https://affiliate-program.amazon.com/influencers
ShopStyle	Helping content creators of all types make money through sponsored content and product recommendations (affiliate program with thousands of brands).	https://www.shopstylecollective.com
Genflow	Genflow is a platform that allows influencers to own their own	https://genflow.com/gca

	audience and build their own brands.	
FamePick	FamePick provides digital creators with business tools to land brand deals and manage their paid content projects from pitch to payment.	https://www.famepick.com
QuikPlace	QuikPlace allows teams and individuals to promote their music or brand on TikTok, Instagram, YouTube, and Twitter all in one place on the world's first public influencer marketplace.	https://quikplace.io
CreatorIQ	The CreatorIQ platform offers a wide range of influencer marketing tools designed to help brands of all sizes, and from all industries.	https://www.creatoriq.com
GRIN	Creator management platform, turning brands into household names through the power of authentic content creator relationships.	https://grin.co

Merchandise/Print-on-demand fulfillment

CafePress	Custom t-shirts, stickers, posters, coffee mugs and more.	https://www.cafepress.com
Teespring	Free platform that lets you create and sell over 50 kinds of products with no upfront cost or risk.	https://teespring.com
RedBubble	Sell uncommon designs on high-quality, everyday products such as apparel, stationery, housewares, bags, wall art and so on.	https://www.redbubble.com
Amazon KDP	KDP allows you to self-publish eBooks, paperbacks, and hardcover books for free.	https://kdp.amazon.com

Membership/Premium Content platforms

Patreon	Patreon is the best place for creators to build memberships by providing exclusive access to their work and a deeper connection with their communities.	https://www.patreon.com
Ko-fi	Ko-fi allows creators to receive money from fans. Anyone who clicks your link can support you with a 'Ko-fi' (a small payment roughly the price of a	https://ko-fi.com

	coffee).	
Podia	Podia is an online platform that allows users to create and sell online courses, memberships, and downloads. It also supports webinars and has some basic community functions that allow users to create content and join discussions based on a course they're taking.	https://www.podia.com
Sellfy	Sellfy is an all-in-one e-commerce service designed for creators to sell digital and/or physical products, digital subscriptions or Print-on-demand merchandise online in a simple way.	https://sellfy.com
Buy Me A Coffee	A free, fast, and meaningful way to accept support and memberships from your fans.	https://www.buymeacoffee.com
Hypage	Generate revenue by creating a landing page for your bio link. Sell your digital products and Set up your membership to monetize your traffic.	https://hypage.com
OnlyFans	OnlyFans is a subscription-	https://onlyfans.com

	based social media platform where users can sell and/or purchase original content. Most people think it's just for adult content, but that's simply not true. Content is mainly created by YouTubers, fitness trainers, models, content creators and public figures in order to monetise their profession.	
Mighty Networks	A Mighty Network includes all the online community features you'd expect: content and a dynamic activity feed; member profiles; conversations and comments; sharing to social media; articles; polls, questions, and posts; events; direct messaging between members; and more.	https://www.mightynetworks.com
Uscreen	Uscreen is a video on demand service that enables anyone to easily build video streaming and subscription channels and sell their content online.	https://www.uscreen.tv
Facebook Creator Studio	Creator Studio brings together all the tools you	https://www.facebook.com/creators

	need to effectively post, manage, monetize and measure content across all your Facebook Pages and Instagram accounts. It also helps you take advantage of new features and monetization opportunities when they become available	
Memberful	Memberful provides an intuitive payment and account management experience for your members which means you'll spend less time providing customer support. Once you create your membership Plans, your audience can buy subscriptions to those Plans and manage their own membership accounts.	https://memberful.com
MemberPress	MemberPress is a WordPress membership site plugin and LMS that makes it easy to charge your users for access to content and digital products such as software, e-books, and online courses you create.	https://memberpress.com

Gumroad	Gumroad is a powerful, but simple, e-commerce platform. We make it easy to earn your first dollar online by selling digital products, memberships and more.	https://gumroad.com
Substack	Substack lets independent writers and podcasters publish directly to their audience and get paid through subscriptions.	https://substack.com
Supercast	Supercast is the podcast subscription platform for thousands of podcasters, networks & publishers. Our top 10 podcasters earn $12+ million a year directly from their listeners.	https://www.supercast.com

Affiliate Marketing

Amazon Associates	The Amazon Associates Program helps content creators, publishers and bloggers monetize their traffic.	https://affiliate-program.amazon.com
Clickbank	Clickbank is both a marketplace for affiliates and an e-commerce platform for digital content creators.	https://www.clickbank.com

ShareASale	ShareASale is a great option for bloggers, content creators, writers, social media marketers, and others in the online marketing space who want to make some extra money recommending their favorite products.	https://www.shareasale.com
Awin (Formerly Affiliate Window)	Awin is a specialist affiliate marketing platform. Our role is to connect our advertisers with a network of publishers from a variety of sectors - price comparison, blogs, social networks and communities, email marketing, display etc, both locally and internationally.	https://www.awin.com/us
PartnerStack	PartnerStack is an ideal platform and marketplace to manage affiliate and partnership marketing programs, especially for B2B SaaS.	https://partnerstack.com
CJ Affiliate (Formerly Commission Junction)	A popular affiliate network for anyone looking to earn passive income with affiliate marketing.	https://www.cj.com
Rakuten Marketing	An affiliate prospecting program that focused on building strong relationships with publishers and educating	https://rakutenadvertising.com

	them on the products offered.	
Avangate Affiliate Network	Digital goods affiliate marketing network designed to help you achieve sustainable growth for your online sales.	https://www.avangate network.com
FlexOffers	FlexOffers is an affiliate marketing network providing comprehensive solutions to publishers and advertisers via multiple strategic options.	https://www.flexoffers. com
Walmart Affiliates	A way for you to earn commissions by placing banner ads or text links on your website to refer customers to Walmart.com.	https://affiliates.walma rt.com
eBay Partner Network	Earn money by driving traffic and prompting sales across one of the world's largest and most diverse marketplaces.	https://partnernetwork .ebay.com

Funnel Creation and Hosting

ClickFunnels	ClickFunnels gives you everything you need to market, sell, and deliver your products and services online!	https://www.clickfunnel s.com
SamCart	Create an eCommerce storefront with SamCart, an easy shopping cart	https://www.samcart.co m

	software and 1-page funnel system, making it simple to sell online.	
Leadpages	Engineered to be the easiest, most effective online website builder, Leadpages sites help you transform web traffic into leads and sales.	https://www.leadpages.com
GetResponse	Powerful, simplified tool to send emails, create pages, and automate your marketing.	https://www.getresponse.com
Builderall	Builderall offers tools to create sites, blogs, automate marketing campaigns, and boost conversion rates.	https://builderall.com
OptimizePress	OptimizePress is a powerful WordPress based software for creating pages and websites for marketing your business. These include landing pages, opt-in pages, webinar registration pages, thank you pages, sales pages.	https://www.optimizepress.com
Systeme	Systeme.io (pronounced "system dot I-O") is an all-in-one online marketing	https://systeme.io

	platform that makes it easy to launch, grow, and scale your online business.	
ActiveCampaign	ActiveCampaign provides cloud-based marketing and sales automation software with features for email marketing, lead scoring and web analytics, a CRM platform, and a live chat messaging platform called Conversations.	https://www.activecampaign.com
Wishpond	Wishpond is a lead generation and marketing automation solution. Featuring a drag-and-drop landing page editor, social contests, popups, and forms, Wishpond features tools for website and email subscriber engagement. Lead scoring, nurturing tools, and performance metrics are also available with this solution.	https://www.wishpond.com
Keap	Keap is an easy-to-use CRM platform with helpful features to organize leads, automate repetitive tasks and get paid faster without third-party tools.	https://keap.com
Unbounce	Unbounce helps you get	https://unbounce.com

	more outta your marketing. From pre-optimized landing pages to great copy that's written for you, we pair your know-how with AI to help you transform your ideas into campaigns that get results.	
ConvertKit	ConvertKit is a full-featured email service provider (ESP). Thanks to its ease of use, automation and other features, it's one of the fastest-growing email marketing companies around. It also offers customizable sign-up forms and landing pages to help bring in more email subscribers.	https://convertkit.com
GrooveFunnels	GrooveFunnels is a complete suite of marketing tools designed to help you build sales funnels and websites (i.e., landing pages) and for selling products online.	https://groovefunnels.com
Kartra	Kartra is an all-in-one marketing platform that lets you build sales funnels, manage marketing campaigns, host	https://home.kartra.com

	online courses, automate comprehensive email sequences, and manage affiliate programs.	
Convertflow	ConvertFlow is an all-in-one platform for converting website visitors. Launch and A/B test landing pages, multi-step popups, sticky bars, quizzes, surveys, site messages, and forms - without coding or developers.	https://www.convertflow.com
Kajabi	Kajabi is an all-in-one business platform for knowledge entrepreneurs. Kajabi makes it easy to build, market and sell your online courses, membership sites, coaching program, and more. Best of all, you won't need to learn code or have to worry about plugins or broken integrations.	https://kajabi.com

Website Hosting

Kinsta (Very Popular ⏺)	Kinsta is a dedicated WordPress hosting company that offers high-	https://kinsta.com

	end performance through Google's C2 cloud computing platform.	
WebHosting Pad	WebHostingPad is a leader in affordable and secure web hosting solutions, offering a free domain, easy-to-use website builders, and 24/7 support.	https://www.webhostingpad.com
BlueHost	Bluehost is one of the largest website hosting providers and powers millions of websites.	https://www.bluehost.com
A2 Hosting	A 99.98% uptime guarantee, free automated backups, and free site migration are only some of the features that set A2 apart as far as reliable web hosting goes. As one of the oldest providers on the market, it's a solid option for both new and veteran websites.	https://www.a2hosting.com
iPage	iPage is a full-service domain and web hosting provider targeting smaller businesses that want to jump into the e-commerce arena.	https://www.ipage.com
Liquid Web	Liquid Web is a Managed	https://www.liquidweb.co

	Hosting provider offering reliable virtual private servers, dedicated servers, and private cloud hosting servers with 24/7/365 Support.	m
BionicWP	BionicWP provides highly customizable managed WordPress hosting. The only TRULY MANAGED WordPress platform for freelancers, businesses, agencies, and super-heroes.	https://www.bionicwp.com
Scala Hosting	ScalaHosting offers SSD (solid state drive) storage, which allows users to access your website faster. Your storage capacity includes all of your website's files, databases and email.	https://www.scalahosting.com
Namecheap	Namecheap began in 2000 with a mission to deliver the best domains at the best prices with the best service. Since then we've added hosting, security, managed WordPress, and a whole range of innovations to our platform.	https://www.namecheap.com

Education and Skill Promotion

LearnWorlds	LearnWorlds is a powerful, easy-to-use and reliable training solution for individuals and enterprises. A fully customizable, white-label solution to train employees and associates, educate customers, or sell online courses to a wide audience.	https://www.learnworlds.com
Udemy	Udemy is an online learning and teaching marketplace with over 213000 courses and 57 million students. Learn programming, marketing, data science and more.	https://www.udemy.com
LinkedIn Learning (Lynda)	LinkedIn Learning is an on-demand library of videos covering business, technology and creative skills. It provides personalized course recommendations to help you achieve your full potential.	https://learning.linkedin.com
Coursera	Coursera is an online learning platform offering self-paced guided projects and on-demand courses on a variety of subjects. The platform partners with universities and companies, including Amazon Web Services, Google and IBM, to provide	https://www.coursera.org

	courses.	
Skillshare	Skillshare is an online learning community for students to take online video classes at their own pace.	https://www.skillshare.com/en/
MasterClass	MasterClass offers online classes created for students of all skill levels. Our instructors are the best in the world.	https://www.masterclass.com
Udacity	Udacity is a global, online, lifelong learning platform connecting education to jobs. Udacity works with industry leaders to create project-based online learning programs. These unique collaborations ensure that students learn the technology skills that employers value most.	https://www.udacity.com
Thinkific	Thinkific is a highly rated platform used to create, market, and sell your own online courses or membership sites. The platform has revolutionized how individuals learn online by building a platform designed for both course creators and their audiences.	https://www.thinkific.com

Appendix A

YouTube Channel:

Mastery Media,
https://www.youtube.com/channel/UCxtGrF-CZRsYoT7uL05o_5A

Website:

Mastery Media, http://masterymediagroup.com/

References

1. Shim, J. P., Eastin, M. S., & Larose, R. (2005). Internet uses and gratification: The role of web portals. New Media & Society, 7(3), 323-347.

2. Srinivasan, R., Anderson, R., & Ponnavolu, K. (2002). Customer loyalty in e-commerce: an exploration of its antecedents and consequences. Journal of Retailing, 78(1), 41-50.

3. Statista. (2022). Number of YouTube users worldwide from 2010 to 2022 (in millions). Statista. https://www.statista.com/statistics/254758/number-of-youtube-users-worldwide/

4. Syed, M. (2017). The art of viral marketing: Crafting contagious content. Kogan Page Publishers.

5. Tausch, N., Kuester, S., & Roessner, D. (2015). The effect of brand placement in video content on consumer attitudes and purchase intentions. Journal of Marketing Communications, 21(4), 309-325.

6. Thompson, J. B. (1995). The media and modernity: A social theory of the media. Stanford University Press.

7. Vorderer, P., Klimmt, C., & Ritterfeld, U. (2004). Enjoyment: At the heart of media entertainment. Communication Theory, 14(4), 388-408.

8. Ruggiero, T. E. (2000). Uses and gratifications theory in the 21st century. Mass Communication & Society, 3(1), 3-37.

9. Sandberg, J., & Donelly, R. (2017). The influence of sponsorship on consumer attitudes and purchase intentions: The moderating effect of sponsorship visibility. Journal of Marketing Communications, 23(2), 128-143.

10. Kietzmann, J. H., Hermkens, K., McCarthy, I. P., & Silvestre, B. S. (2011). Social media? Get serious! Understanding the functional building blocks of social media. Business Horizons, 54(3), 241-251.

11. Kotevska, K., Janda, K., & Trajkoska, B. (2018). How to monetize YouTube videos? The influence of video content and YouTube channel characteristics. Telematics and Informatics, 35(4), 1169-1180.

12. Lefebvre, L. C., & Lefebvre, L. (2018). Using YouTube to promote a business: A content analysis of small and medium-sized enterprises. Journal of Business and Technical Communication, 32(3), 375-407.

13. Lum, Y. W., & Chua, R. Y. (2013). Social media marketing: An examination of consumer motivations and barriers. Journal of Interactive Marketing, 27(3), 123-130.

14. Ma, Q., & Lee, J. H. (2017). The effects of influencer type and endorsement type on consumer purchase intention in social media. Telematics and Informatics, 34(3), 441-450.

15. Mangold, W. G., & Faulds, D. J. (2009). Social media: The new hybrid element of the promotion mix. Business Horizons, 52(4), 357-365.

16. Martinez, I., & Hermida, A. (2017). YouTube: A new frontier for journalism? How news organizations are using the platform for storytelling. Digital Journalism, 5(3), 316-335.

17. McInerney, J. (2015). The role of YouTube in education: The next generation of education technology. Journal of Educational Technology Development and Exchange, 7(1), 1-5.

18. Musero, A. (2019). Content creation and audience engagement on YouTube: An analysis of Spanish YouTubers. Digital Journalism, 7(6), 667-683.

19. Oliver, M. B. (2017). Why brands use influencer marketing: Evidence from firms that use influencer marketing. International Journal of Advertising, 36(1), 56-70.

20. Parsons, J., & Fisher, K. E. (2018). The YouTube personality phenomenon: An examination of the role of YouTube personalities in shaping consumer behavior. Journal of Consumer Behavior, 17(3), 170-178.

21. Prentice, R. (2017). From broadcast to narrowcast: A case study of YouTube as a political news source. New Media & Society, 19(1), 36-53.

22. Qu, Y., & Lu, L. (2016). Why people use social media: An examination of the benefits of social media usage. International Journal of Human-Computer Interaction, 32(3), 199-208.

23. Rosen, L. D., Carrier, L. M., & Cheever, N. A. (2014). The Social Information Processing Model of Internet Addiction: Theoretical foundations, empirical evidence, and future directions. Cyberpsychology, Behavior, and Social Networking, 17(5), 269-277.

24. Bughin, J., & Chui, M. (2018). Ten implications for digital strategies in the age of artificial intelligence. McKinsey & Company. https://www.mckinsey.com/business-functions/digital-mckinsey/our-insights/ten-implications-for-digital-strategies-in-the-age-of-artificial-intelligence

25. Green, T. (2017). The Complete Guide to YouTube Marketing. Kogan Page Publishers.

26. Pew Research Center. (2018). YouTube, Instagram, Snapchat usage continues to rise. Pew Research Center. https://www.pewresearch.org/fact-tank/2018/10/30/youtube-instagram-snapchat-usage-continues-to-rise/

27. Yang, Q., & Chen, W. (2015). A study of the YouTube phenomenon in China. Telematics and Informatics, 32(2), 185-194. https://doi.org/10.1016/j.tele.2014.07.001

28. Chen, Y., & Liang, X. (2017). YouTube Influencer Marketing: A review of the literature. International Journal of Information Management, 37(1), 1-10. https://doi.org/10.1016/j.ijinfomgt.2017.05.003

29. Vorderer, P., Klimmt, C., & Ritterfeld, U. (2004). Enjoyment: At the heart of media entertainment. Communication Theory, 14(4), 388-408. https://doi.org/10.1111/j.1468-2885.2004.tb00310.x

30. Meenaghan, T. (2011). Influencer marketing: A new form of word of mouth marketing. Journal of Advertising Research, 51(2), 305-312. https://doi.org/10.2501/JAR-51-2-305-312

31. Grier, S., & Böck, A. (2010). A critical review of YouTube: Opportunities and challenges for online video distribution. Journal of Information Technology & Politics, 7(3), 191-208. https://doi.org/10.1080/19331680903298166

32. Keating, B., & Slater, M. D. (2011). Selective self-presentation in computer-mediated communication: Hyperpersonal dimensions of technology, language, and cognition. Computers in Human

Behavior, 27(3), 748-760.
https://doi.org/10.1016/j.chb.2010.11.019

33. Bauer, M. W., & Gaskell, G. (2000). Towards a paradigm shift in research on social representations. European Journal of Social Psychology, 30(1), 1-16. https://doi.org/10.1002/(SICI)1099-0992(200001/02)30:1<1::AID-EJSP1>3.0.CO;2-7

Afterword

Writing this book has been a journey, and I am grateful for the opportunity to share my story and my knowledge with you, the reader. I hope that the insights and advice shared within these pages have provided you with a roadmap for starting and growing your own successful YouTube channel.

The road to success on YouTube is never easy, but with hard work and determination, it is possible. Remember that success takes time, and that the journey is just as important as the destination. Don't be discouraged by setbacks, and don't be afraid to pivot and try new things.

Most importantly, always stay true to yourself and your passions. Your unique voice and perspective are what make your content special, and what will help you build a loyal and engaged audience.

Thank you for reading this book, and I wish you all the best in your journey towards creating a successful YouTube channel. If you have any questions or feedback, please don't hesitate to reach out. I would love to hear from you and support you in any way I can.

With gratitude, Matthew Wheeler

www.ingramcontent.com/pod-product-compliance
Lightning Source LLC
La Vergne TN
LVHW051246050326
832903LV00028B/2601